# Brad Birch

# Plays: 1

## Where the Shot Rabbits Lay; Even Stillness Breathes Softly Against a Brick Wall; The Brink; Black Mountain

*Where the Shot Rabbits Lay*: 'There are some lovely grace notes in Brad Birch's intimate father-son tale.' *Time Out London*

*Even Stillness Breathes Softly Against a Brick Wall*: 'A lovely play of sharp edges, falsehoods and unsaid thoughts, twinning great humour and strong emotion throughout.' *WhatsOnStage*

*The Brink*: 'Short, sharp, shockingly entertaining.' *Guardian*

*Black Mountain*: 'This is a real rarity.' *Scotsman*

**Brad Birch** is a Welsh playwright whose work has been produced by the Royal Court, Sherman Cymru, Soho Theatre, Orange Tree Theatre and Paines Plough, and performed in Russia, the USA, Malta and Spain. His theatre work includes *Black Mountain* for Paines Plough, Theatr Clwyd and the Orange Tree; *This Must be the Place* for Poleroid at the VAULT Festival; *The Brink* at the Orange Tree; *The Endless Ocean* at the RWCMD; *Tender Bolus* at the Royal Exchange and Schauspielhaus, Hamburg; *Gardening for the Unfulfilled and Alienated* for Undeb at the Edinburgh Festival; *Soap Opera*, *Where the Shot Rabbits Lay* and *Permafrost* at the Royal Court; *Even Stillness Breathes Softly Against a Brick Wall* at Soho Theatre; *Light Arrested Between the Curtain and the Glass* at Sherman Cymru. His collaboration with Kenny Emson won the Pick of the Year Award at the VAULT festival in 2017, and he won the Harold Pinter Commission in 2016 and the Fringe First Award in 2013. He is currently under commission at the Royal Shakespeare Company and Royal Court.

T0353553

# Brad Birch

# Plays: 1

**Where the Shot Rabbits Lay**
**Even Stillness Breathes Softly Against a Brick Wall**
**The Brink**
**Black Mountain**

*With an introduction by the author*

*methuen* | drama

LONDON · NEW YORK · OXFORD · NEW DELHI · SYDNEY

METHUEN DRAMA
Bloomsbury Publishing Plc
50 Bedford Square, London, WC1B 3DP, UK

BLOOMSBURY, METHUEN DRAMA and the Methuen Drama logo are
trademarks of Bloomsbury Publishing Plc

This collection published in Great Britain 2018

*Where the Shot Rabbits Lay* first published in
this collection by Methuen Drama 2018

Copyright © Brad Birch, 2018

*Even Stillness Breathes Softly Against a Brick Wall*
first published by Methuen Drama 2013

Copyright © Brad Birch, 2013

*The Brink* first published by Methuen Drama 2016

Copyright © Brad Birch, 2016

*Black Mountain* first published by Methuen Drama 2017

Copyright © Brad Birch, 2017

Brad Birch has asserted his right under the Copyright, Designs
and Patents Act, 1988, to be identified as author of this work.

Cover design: Olivia D'Cruz

Cover image © Jim West/Alamy Stock Photo

A catalogue record for this book is available from the British Library.

A catalog record for this book is available from the Library of Congress.

ISBN: PB: 978-1-350-07530-6
ePDF: 978-1-350-07532-0
eBook: 978-1-350-07534-4

Series: Contemporary Dramatists

Typeset by Mark Heslington Ltd, Scarborough, North Yorkshire

To find out more about our authors and books visit *www.bloomsbury.com*
and sign up for our *newsletters*.

# Contents

# Introduction

I grew up in the spa town of Llandrindod Wells, near the border between Wales and England. A large (for that part of the world) town that once functioned as a holistic retreat for the Victorian rich and unwell, it now serves as the civic and commercial centre for the flecks and smatterings of farming communities in Mid Wales. In lots of instances, the border between places often exists as the most active site of difference. It is, by definition, the limit; a space of territory and contestation. But that wasn't so much the case for us growing up in Powys. For us, existing there felt less like the border between two places, and more like the periphery of anywhere. We weren't quite Welsh enough, and we definitely weren't English. We had a rich history which was made a lot of, but systemic underfunding and neglect meant that the present and the future felt more tired than the past. We'd tend to carry an agricultural burr in our accents, closer to the dialects of Herefordshire or Shropshire than North or South Wales, and the great Welsh battles of language and labour felt received rather than lived.

And I think it's only in the last few years that I've realised the significance of this geography on my understanding of the world and my place within it. This sense of periphery, of existing on the edge of distinction, could map onto almost every experience in my life. And while that's probably a bit too general, exaggerated and contradictory to be true, it functions as quite a useful lens when looking retrospectively at some of the plays that I've written.

This is a collection of young and unsettled plays. They don't quite know what they are. They show a playwright trying to find a form and a language and a story to tell, related in their attempts to exhibit a discomfort with the world that they are in. In each play there is a character or characters whose experience of the world conflicts with what they are being told, or contradicts how the world is being experienced by others. They are unable to cope or manage with the doubts that have unsettled them, pushed them into disorder, and the stories are often stories of these people trying to find order or reconcile these differences of perspective.

It was during the Young Writers Programme in 2010, and under the tutelage of Leo Butler, that I wrote the play *Where the Shot Rabbits Lay*. It wasn't the first play I'd written, but it was perhaps the first play I properly thought about before I started typing. Before then, my writing was feverish and instinctive, and once I'd gotten everything out I'd then inefficiently work backwards and try to find a sense in what was there. Leo guided me towards thinking about structure, tempo and control. Signing on and living back with my parents, I was able to invest a lot of time in this and I'd write towards the weekly sessions, returning to the Court with a few pages or an idea or even a draft to show Leo.

The journeys there started on Monday morning, taking the 6.50 am train from Llandrindod Wells towards Shrewsbury, changing at Craven Arms and then at Newport, before arriving in London near to midday. At the end of the session I'd then get the very last train out of Paddington at around 10.30 pm. I'd always have a two-hour wait at Swansea between 2 am and 4 am, and I'd spend this time sat on the benches on the platform, with the station technically closed, either reading a play that Leo had lent me, or writing notes or bits of scenes. I'd arrive back in Llandrindod Wells at 6.50 am on the Tuesday morning, in a satisfactorily neat, but profoundly knackering, round trip.

I was interested in writing a play about two characters who were either mirrors of each other, or functioned as a call and response. I thought that there was something abstract and Beckettian about that. Leo encouraged me to ground this idea and I ended up with a father and son. I was reading a lot of Robert Holman at the time and was interested in the gesture of characters on stage for whom the act of communication is a struggle. The play, therefore, exists in the white bits on the page and in our interpretation of the characters' acknowledged inability to say what they want. Their dialogue gives us clues, and we construct the meaning. This process was instrumental in my understanding of writing dialogue – that characters react not just to what is said, but in what they think the other character is trying to do with what they're saying. It allows aspects of the play to exist on the subterranean. Both characters are trying to negotiate their own feelings with the performative roles they feel they have to meet. The man is dogged by a belief that he can never live up to his idea of being a good father, and the boy sits awkwardly between fascination and anger with his estranged dad.

Music was probably the first art form that I felt creatively inspired by. While I had been a big fan of the films of Steve Martin and John Candy, they never triggered something within me that compelled me to want to do what they did. I remember being around 11 or 12 and my dad introducing me to the Velvet Underground and Jimi Hendrix. There was something about the cosmic opulence of Hendrix and the barbarism of Lou Reed's song-writing that caused an almost obsessional and definitely physical response. From that moment, music became, and probably still is, the art form that means the most to me. I would go on to form my own tastes and interests, but my dad was the gateway and therefore the architect of the metric by which I valued and understood music.

Later, in my early twenties and as a member of the Young Writers Programme, I came to terms with the devastating notion that I would never write songs like The Fall or Magazine. I did realise that I could, however, if I tried very hard, write text that imitated or evoked what those songs did to me. In its form, *Even Stillness Breathes Softly Against a Brick Wall* is almost the exact opposite to anything else I had written up until that point, but the gesture of it felt true to my formative experiences listening to my dad's post-punk and garage rock cassettes. The first incarnation of this story was as a poem with two voices in it. Leo Butler encouraged me to keep writing and find the play within it.

The themes of this play have determined a lot of what I'm interested in now. I'm conscious of conceptions of the Good Life and how ingrained certain beliefs and fears are in our culture. I was conscious of the unique precarity of being young in twenty-first-century Britain. An abundance of almost-free information contradicted the scarcity of space and substance that many of us found ourselves experiencing. The play attempted to articulate the frustrated and often lonely alienation and anxiety that the young modern world fostered. I was interested in how, rapidly, the boundary between work and life seemed to be smudged into a blur; how a culture of customisation and individualisation meant that collective experience was often a rare and uncomfortable event, often caused by accident; and an ideology (demonstrated by the dominance of a particular kind of technology – a phone which has no dedicated off switch) was softly pushing us towards a near-constant invitation to engage and absorb and consume.

The play was directly inspired by the simultaneous messages coming out of the mainstream media at the time, telling us to be alert to the potential dangers of terrorism, while also telling us to 'keep calm and carry on'. These seemingly contradictory messages made sense to me as a call to politely brace ourselves for annihilation. But it was also cleverer than that. I was living in Brighton at the time and was struck by the prevailing trend for kitsch and homely design and television programming, while at the same time we were being asked by our government to accept a near-permanent state of threat. I remember how the large billboards at Brighton train station would regularly advertise baking and gardening programmes with national colours, bunting and primness. And I remember also at the same time how the tannoys would repeat calls for passengers to be vigilant against suspicious behaviour. I realised that perhaps these two things weren't as unrelated as they were disconcerting.

That they, in a sense, came together. That the current taste wasn't just for mindless nostalgia, it was orchestrated with a purpose. It was a nostalgia for the conditions of war. We were harking back to an era when we had an enemy we could see, we could fight, we could unreservedly despise.

The characters in *Even Stillness* . . . are screaming, they're desperate for help. Their calls are not listened to and they fall apart. It was important for me that they were articulate and self-aware. They could have a relationship with the audience. In the same way that the disposition of the characters in *Shot Rabbits* determined the form of that play, the characters in this determined how *Even Stillness* . . . was told.

While formally very different (and indeed different from each other), the next two plays, *The Brink* and *Black Mountain*, are informed by the same concerns. They are plays about the drift, disconnect and disintegration of human experiences in times of dissonance. Neither Nick in *The Brink*, nor Rebecca in *Black Mountain*, can forget what they have learnt – that things in their world are not as they seem, the rules have been broken. Once one brick is dislodged, the whole building falls. They try to find sense and new meaning in this shifting landscape.

I'm currently writing two plays. One is an adaptation and the other is an original story. They both speak to my ongoing interests – how we deal with the unreality of our world, how we cope with technological and ideological pressures against our agency and how we exist in space together. But as with the plays in this collection, they are formally quite different from each other, and I wonder whether I will ever settle on a particular way of telling stories. So far, I've found it interesting to flit about, to look from one angle and then another. Whether considered together or as four different attempts at tackling the same thing, I think the plays in this collection give a good account of a period of time in the world and in my life when I was writing.

There are so many people I want to thank. The directors Nick Bagnall, Nadia Latif, Mel Hillyard and James Grieve for bringing these plays to life and the companies at The Royal Court, Soho Theatre, Paines Plough and the Orange Tree. Chris Campbell for his advice, warmth and advocacy over these years. Leo Butler, Simon Stephens and Mark Ravenhill for their support, friendship and mentorship. Giles Smart, for being the most brilliant agent and support. Anna Brewer and Dom O'Hanlon at Methuen Drama. Peter Cox, for introducing me to playwrighting back in Mid Wales, for sharing his books and insight and inspiration. Andrew Sterry and Ian Yeoman, for giving me my first opportunities as a playwright. My friends Kenny Emson, Luke Barnes, Al Smith, Declan Feenan and John O'Donovan for their years of encouragement. My parents, who have always unconditionally supported my writing, who allowed me to take risks and invested so much of their own time and energy into my work. I'm so very bloody grateful.

And of course Zoe, my partner, and Woody, my son. We became a family with the arrival of Woody at the end of 2015. Life can be very daunting and humbling and exciting, and I'm very glad that I'm doing it with these people. This collection is for them.

*London, winter 2018*

# Where The Shot Rabbits Lay

**Characters**

**Man**
**Boy**

**Set**

*A forest*

**Note on the text**

*( . . .) denotes speech trailing off*

*(/) and (\) denotes interruption*

*Punctuation is to suggest delivery rather than conform to the rules of grammar*

*Beats < Pauses < Silences*

## One

*A small patch of land deep within a forest.*

*The sun filters through bracken and trees. The ground still damp from the morning dew.*

*Footsteps are heard coming towards the space. Two people. Branches breaking underfoot.*

*The* **Man** *enters, carrying a tent bag, rucksack and general camping equipment.*

**Man**   What about here?
  The sun comes through the trees.
  Bit damp but that's alright.
  What do you think?

*The* **Boy** *follows, carrying a rucksack and a coolbox.*

**Boy**   Don't know.

**Man**   They look thick enough to give us some shelter.
  The trees.
  Won't keep us dry.
  Won't get pissed wet through, either.

**Boy**   Isn't that what the tent's for?

**Man**   When we're in it.

*Beat.*

  Well, I like it.
  I don't mind it here.
  It's a good spot.
  What do you think?

**Boy**   I don't know.

**Man**   You don't know what?

**Boy**   I don't know if it's good or not.

**Man**   Why?
  What's wrong with it?

**Boy**   Nothing.
I don't know.

**Man**   Well how do you feel about it?
Do you mind it here?

**Boy**   It's alright.

**Man**   Good.
*It's alright.*
Well, that's enough.

*Pause.*

Hey, do you think we could see
the stars from here?

**Boy**   Not when it's day.

**Man**   No, I know not when it's day.
I mean at night.
I mean that break in the trees.
We could sit under it when it's dry.
Watch the stars.

*Beat.*

What do you think?

**Boy**   Suppose.

**Man**   Suppose, yeah.
I suppose so too.

*Pause.*

You can put the bag down.

*The **Man** starts searching the area.*

You know my old man used to bring me
out camping too.
Something special about it.
Something natural.

**Boy**   Here?

**Man**    What?

**Boy**    You want me to leave it here?

**Man**    Anywhere. Yeah.

*The **Boy** puts the bags and coolbox on the floor.*

Don't suppose you get to go out camping
much at home?

**Boy**    No.

**Man**    It's why I moved back here, you know.
I missed nature.
Your mother was never keen on the outdoors.

*Beat.*

I don't suppose she's ever taken you out like this?

**Boy**    No.

**Man**    No. Well . . .

**Boy**    Too busy having to work.

*Pause.*

**Man**    Look, we better get set up.

**Boy**    Is that all you look for, then?

**Man**    What?

**Boy**    The view of the stars.
Is that all that matters?

**Man**    Yeah. No.
Well.
To me, it is.
But no, I suppose it doesn't matter.
Nothing does, really.
It's up to you.

**Boy**    Nothing matters?

**Man**   What are you looking for?
Designated areas?

**Boy**   The sign for designated areas is over there.

**Man**   I don't care where the sign is.

*Pause.*

You know you do too much of that.

**Boy**   Too much of what?

**Man**   Already.
All we've done is drive down here.
You're worrying.
You're a worrier.
It's all good.
This is nature.
Not one of the campsites.
That's not real.
This is raw.
This is camping.

*Beat.*

Can you pass me that bag?

*The **Boy** passes him the tent bag.*


**Two**

*Moments later.*

*The patch.*

*The **Man** lies the ground cloth down on the floor.*

*He lays out the poles, the stakes, etc.*

*The **Boy** watches.*

**Man**   Do you want to learn how to pitch a tent?

**Boy**   OK.

**Man**    Come here.
So you can see.

*The **Man** stops what he is doing.*

*He gets up and demonstrates.*

Now, you need the land pretty flat.
You want it flat.
First thing you should look for.
A flat space.

**Boy**    Is this flat?

**Man**    Yeah, pretty flat.

**Boy**    It slopes a bit.

**Man**    Yeah, it does slope a bit.
But if we have it so our heads are facing uphill
then we'll be alright.
It doesn't really matter, I suppose.

*Beat.*

So once you've checked the land
you're pitching on . . .
You know what pitching means?

**Boy**    Yeah.

**Man**    It means where you put up your tent.
Pitching is like putting up.

**Boy**    Yeah.

**Man**    So before you pitch your tent
you check the space for sharp objects.
Glass or sticks or pine cones or conker shells.
Sharp objects.

**Boy**    And did you do that?

**Man**    Yeah.
    Yeah, a bit.
    It looked alright.

*Beat.*

    So then you lay the ground cloth.
    Don't really have to worry about straightening it out.
    The corners can just . . .
    So then you get the body of the tent.
    The body.
    Will you pass me the body?

**Boy**    The main bit?

**Man**    The main bit is the body, yes.

**Boy** *takes the body of the tent and passes it to the* **Man**.

*The* **Boy** *then proceeds to follow the instruction of the* **Man**. *He describes what they do as they do it.*

    Now you lay this bit on top.
    But grab the corners.
    Pull the corners out.
    Good yeah.
    We've got to put the poles together.
    They go across the . . .
    across the top bit here.
    Watch because they can snap together.
    Be careful.
    The pole connection can . . . it can fray a bit.
    Are you alright?

**Boy**    What?

**Man**    Are you alright?

*Pause.*

**Boy**    Yeah.

**Man**    Yeah.
  Good.
  Right.

*Beat.*

  So you insert the pole ends
  into the corners of the tent.
  The corners have gromits
  so we can put them in there.
  Like that.
  You'd tell me if you wasn't alright?

**Boy**    Yeah.

**Man**    Good.
  Connect one side and then the other side.
  Diagonally.
  I'll do this diagonal.
  You do that one.
  See what I mean?
  So it can cross over.

**Boy**    Yeah.

**Man**    Good.
  Right.
  So now we can put the tent up.
  The canopy has clips.
  So clip them to the poles.
  Insert the middle pole.
  Right over the top of the crossing poles.
  And then where they cross we clip them there.
  Check the gromits.
  Right.
  Are they secure?

**Boy**    What?

**Man**    Are the gromits secure?

**Boy**    These?

**Man**   Yes as I said they are the gromits.
 Are they secure?

**Boy**   Yeah.

**Man**   Are you sure?

**Boy**   Yes.

**Man**   Good.
 Right, so if it rains
 then we need another sheet on top.
 The outside sheet there.

**Boy**   The what?

**Man**   Outside sheet.

**Boy**   Is that what it's called?

**Man**   I don't know what's it called proper.
 *Vestibule*, maybe.
 It doesn't matter.
 The window's always at the front.
 So we stake these down.
 Pass me the hammer.

*The* **Boy** *gets the hammer.*

 We angle the stakes at about 45 degrees.
 So they really . . .
 you know . . .
 dig in.
 But I can do them.

*Beat.*

 That's it.
 That's how you put up a tent.

**Boy**   Right.

*Pause.*

 Who taught you?

**Man**    Nobody.

**Boy**    How did you learn?

**Man**    I just did it.
I learnt as I went.

**Boy**    No one showed you?

**Man**    Well, Granddad was there.
But this was my job.
He didn't do the tent.

**Boy**    How did you know you were doing it right?

**Man**    Because it never fell down on us.

*Pause.*

Anyway.
I can do this bit.
I can do this bit on my own.

**Boy**    Right.

*The* **Boy** *sits back down and watches the* **Man** *hammer the stakes in.*


**Three**

*A short while later.*

*The camp.*

*The tent and bits are completely set up.*

*The* **Man** *and the* **Boy** *are sat opposite each other.*

**Man**    You want anything to drink?

**Boy**    No.

**Man**    You don't want anything?

**Boy**    No. I'm OK.

*Pause.*

**Man**    So I was thinking
we might head out over there tomorrow.
Explore.

**Boy**    Explore?

**Man**    Yeah.

**Boy**    I thought you knew this place.

**Man**    I do.
But you don't.

**Boy**    But I'm with you.

*Pause.*

**Man**    There's a river.

*Beat.*

I thought we could do some hunting.
You ever been shooting?

**Boy**    No.
Shooting what?

**Man**    Well what do you think?
Not going to be shooting gazelles, are we?
Rabbits.
Shooting rabbits.

**Boy**    Right.

**Man**    We could do that.
If you want.

*Pause.*

Are you sure you don't want anything?

**Boy**    Yeah.

**Man**    We've got things.
If you wanted something to eat.

**Boy**    I don't.

**Man**   Boys are always eating.
When I was your age I was always eating.
You know
you used to have such an appetite on you
when you were a kid.

**Boy**   Did I?

**Man**   Yeah.

*Silence.*

Do you drink beer?

**Boy**   Not really.

**Man**   Not really?
You either do or you don't.

**Boy**   Then I don't.

*Pause.*

**Man**   It's not a trick question.
I brought beer.

*He searches through the coolbox. He takes out some cans.*

See?

**Boy**   No.

**Man**   No what?

**Boy**   No, thank you.

**Man**   No, I mean *no* what?
You don't see or you don't want a beer?

**Boy**   I don't want a beer.

*Silence.*

**Man**   If you're worried about your mother . . .
She won't find out.

**Boy**   I'm not worried.

**Man**   If you were worried about what she might say.

**Boy**   I don't care.

**Man**   She does things.
She says things.
I know she does.
But she does and says them to protect you.
I want to protect you too.
A beer with me is OK.

**Boy**   She lets me have beer.

*Beat.*

I just don't like it.

**Man**   You don't?

**Boy**   No.

*Pause.*

**Man**   So you've drank beer.

**Boy**   I'm not twelve.

**Man**   No.
Course.

*Silence.*

**Boy**   Do you have coke?

**Man**   Coke?

**Boy**   Yeah, just a can of coke or something?

**Man**   Oh.
Course I've . . .
Yeah mate.
I've got coke.

*He searches through the coolbox.*

*He finds a coke.*

*He passes the* **Boy** *a coke.*

**Boy**    Thanks.

**Man**    You like coke.
We've got plenty of coke.

**Four**

*A little later.*

*The camp.*

*The* **Man** *is fashioning a walking stick by shaving the bark off a large, fallen branch with a penknife.*

*The* **Boy** *watches.*

**Man**    You know the different trees round here?

**Boy**    No.

**Man**    Well you can tell that that's a Leyland Cypress.
Look at the funny shaped leaves.

**Boy**    Right.

**Man**    You don't climb a Leyland Cypress.

**Boy**    Why not?

**Man**    The branches are too weak.
Look at this.
This kind of branch is better for climbing.

**Boy**    What tree is that from?

**Man**    Well this is an oak, isn't it?

**Boy**    I don't know.

**Man**    Look at how the leaves fan a little.

**Boy**    Right.

**Man**    You see?

**Boy**   Yeah.

**Man**   That's an oak.

*Pause.*

When I was young.
Younger than you.
A kid.
Back on the farm.
Your granddad's house.
You know the old house?

**Boy**   Yeah.

**Man**   Out the back.
Far out.
The other side of the farm.
There was the lake.
You know the lake?

**Boy**   No.

**Man**   No?

*Beat.*

We never took you down there?

**Boy**   No.

**Man**   Oh.

**Boy**   Mum didn't like me going off out
when we visited Nan.
She didn't like me out on the farm.

**Man**   No.
I suppose she didn't.

*Pause.*

I'll have to take you down there.
Next time I go down I'll take you
and we'll go to the lake.
It's still there.

**Boy**   You'd take me on your own?

**Man**   Yeah.
  Why not?

*Silence.*

  What was I talking about?
  The lake.
  I was telling you about the lake, wasn't I?
  It was great.
  Real pure.
  Real clean.
  Not like some of these swampy lakes you can get.
  It had a fresh crisp to it on hot days.
  Your nan never liked me going there.
  Like your mother with you.
  But, you know, I went anyway.
  In the summer, when it was hot, I went anyway.

**Boy**   She never caught you?

**Man**   Well, it wasn't like she'd ever be out that far.
  She'd never just walk up there.
  I would swim then dry off on the rocks in the sun.
  Your nan didn't have a clue.
  Of course, in those days we still had hot summers.

*Pause.*

  Could drown in that lake.
  Almost did.

**Boy**   Really?

**Man**   Yeah.
  A couple of times I almost did.
  But, you know, didn't.

*Pause.*

  I could go back there.
  I could go back there now.

*Silence.*

> But I'm here, you see.
> I'm here.
> I wanted to tell you.
> To say that . . .
> Me and your mother . . .
> You know . . .
> I don't think . . .
> I don't want you to think that . . .
> You know?

*Beat.*

> I'm here because of you.
> That goes for your mother, as well.

**Five**

*A while later.*

*The camp.*

*It is now getting darker. Deep orange with a hint of purple skies.*

*The* **Man** *is struggling to start a fire.*

*The* **Boy** *is looking at the rifle.*

**Boy**    Can I have a look at your gun?

**Man**    Yeah course.

**Boy**    Can I pick it up?

**Man**    Yeah.

**Boy**    Wow.

**Man**    What do you think?

**Boy**    It's nice.

**Man**    Yeah.
It is.

**Boy**   It's heavy.

**Man**   It's not heavy.

**Boy**   Heavier than I thought.

**Man**   You get a clean shot with it.
You want to load a shot?

**Boy**   I don't know how.

**Man**   I'll teach you.

*Beat.*

**Boy**   Is it hard to shoot?

**Man**   No.

**Boy**   It looks hard.

**Man**   It isn't.

**Boy**   Who taught you?

**Man**   Granddad.

*Pause.*

**Boy**   How old were you?

**Man**   I don't know.
About your age or so.
Eleven-ish.

**Boy**   I'm thirteen.

**Man**   I said *or so*.

*Silence.*

**Boy**   You ever shoot someone?

**Man**   You mean a person?

**Boy**   Yeah.

**Man**   Have I ever shot a person?

**Boy**   Yeah.

**Man**   Why would I shoot someone?

**Boy**   I don't know.

*Pause.*

**Man**   Do I seem the kind of person
that would shoot someone?

**Boy**   I don't know.
I guess not.

*Pause.*

**Man**   Of course I'm not.


**Six**

*Night time.*

*The camp.*

*The fire is now ablaze.*

*They sit either side of it.*

*The **Man** is lying back, drinking a beer.*

*The **Boy** is sat by the tent, staring at the fire, drinking a coke.*

**Man**   How's school?

**Boy**   OK.

**Man**   Just OK?

**Boy**   It's alright.

**Man**   You working hard?

**Boy**   I suppose.

**Man**   Getting good marks?

**Boy**   Yeah.
  Alright I suppose.

*Pause.*

**Man**   As long as you're trying your best.

**Boy**   Yeah.

**Man**   Good.

*Pause.*

  Still hanging around with that girl?
  What's her name?
  Hannah?

**Boy**   No.

**Man**   No it's not Hannah
  or no you don't hang around with her?

**Boy**   No I don't hang around with her.

**Man**   Oh.
  That's a shame.

*Beat.*

  Well people change.
  It's OK to change.

**Boy**   Yeah I know.

*Pause.*

**Man**   Couldn't split you two up when you were little.
  Good you have girl friends.

**Boy**   I don't have a girlfriend.

**Man**   I meant friends who are girls.

**Boy**   I don't.

**Man**   Why don't you see her anymore?

**Boy**   I was never seeing her.

**Man**   You saw her.

**Boy**   But I wasn't seeing her.

**Man**   That's what I said.

**Boy**   It's not the same thing.

**Man**   What's the difference?

**Boy**   Seeing is when you're with a girl
but you're not going out.

*Pause.*

**Man**   Like a fuck buddy?

**Boy**   A what?

**Man**   A fuck buddy.
It's when you . . .
You've never heard of a fuck buddy?

**Boy**   You've never heard of seeing someone?

**Man**   I'm not thirteen.

**Boy**   But you were.

**Man**   A long time ago.

*Pause.*

**Boy**   Do you have a fuck buddy?

*Beat.*

**Man**   No.

*Pause.*

**Boy**   Does Mum?

*Pause.*

**Man**   I don't know what your mother gets up to.

**Seven**

*The next morning.*

*The camp.*

*They are sat eating breakfast off paper plates.*

*Silence.*

*The* **Man** *finishes.*

*The* **Boy** *finishes.*

**Man**    How was that?

**Boy**    Yeah.

**Man**    Sorry it's just beans, I . . .
Those sausages were the shit ones.
Burn like paper.
Probably made out of paper so cheap.

**Boy**    It's alright.

**Man**    There's a shop up the road.
Get you something better for later.
You finished?

**Boy**    Yeah.

**Man**    Here.
Give us your plate.

**Boy**    Do you want help washing the pan and stuff?

*The* **Man** *gets up and takes his and the* **Boy**'s *plates and puts them by the frying pan.*

**Man**    No.
It's alright.
I'm not washing them yet.

**Boy**    You're not washing up?

**Man**    Not right now, no.

*Beat.*

That OK?

**Boy**   Yeah.

**Man**   I'll do it later.

*Pause.*

You mind me doing it later?

*Beat.*

You want me to do it now?

**Boy**   I don't mind.

*He picks up the frying pan.*

**Man**   Right.
Alright.
I'll do it now.

**Boy**   No.

*He goes to walk away.*

*He stops.*

**Man**   I'm not your mother, you know.
When you're with me we do things differently.
That's the point of having two fucking parents.

*Beat.*

Anyway.
Don't know if I've time.
I didn't think we'd be . . .
I didn't think you'd take so long eating.
We better get going.

**Boy**   Where?

**Man**   Hunting.
Shooting.
Rabbits.
Remember?

**Boy**    Yeah.

**Man**    Yeah.
  Get your things.


**Eight**

*A little later.*

*The forest.*

*They are walking.*

*The **Man** is carrying the gun.*

*The **Boy** is carrying a bag.*

*The **Man** stops to take it all in.*

**Man**    This is it you know.
  This is the stuff.
  I don't like walking.
  Not usually.
  I'm not a walker.
  In town.
  Can't stand it.
  But out here.
  Could go miles.
  I'd never stop.

**Boy**    Yeah.

**Man**    Two men and a gun.
  Something heroic in that.

**Boy**    Yeah.

**Man**    I didn't mean to bite before.
  I just want you to feel comfortable around me.
  Want you to know
  that just because your mother does something
  it doesn't mean it's right.
  It's right most of the time.
  But not always.

*Beat.*

Are you alright?

**Boy**   Yeah.

**Man**   Good.

*The **Man** goes to leave again.*

**Boy**   Can I ask you something?

**Man**   Yeah course.

**Boy**   Shouldn't we have a map?

**Man**   What?

**Boy**   A map.
So we don't get lost?

**Man**   No.
We'll be alright.

**Boy**   I can't remember where we came from.

**Man**   Well we've walked in a straight line.
So if we turn around
and go in the other direction in a straight line
we'll find our camp.
Simple, really.

**Boy**   OK.

*Beat.*

Is it that simple?

**Man**   It can be.

*Silence.*

**Boy**   I really don't know /

**Man**   / Wait.

*The **Man** points to a bush in the middle distance.*

The bush over there.
There.
You see it?

**Boy**   Yeah.

**Man**   You see the rabbit?

**Boy**   Yeah.

**Man**   Watch this.

*The* **Man** *aims the gun.*

*He hesitates.*

**Boy**   You gonna get it?

*He gives the* **Boy** *the gun.*

**Man**   You do it.

**Boy**   I don't know how.

**Man**   I'll show you.

*The* **Boy** *takes the gun.*

Get the butt in the corner of your shoulder.
See it fits in the, that's it.
So it's firm.
Line the gun through with this arm.
Hold the gun down the barrel there.
That's what you're directing the shot with
so keep it straight.
Then the other hand on the trigger there.
Just hold your finger over it.
Follow the sight so it's directly on the rabbit.
You still see the rabbit?

**Boy**   Yeah.

**Man**   You got it?

**Boy**   Yeah.
What do I aim for?

**Man**    The head or the neck.

**Boy**    I can't get the head.

**Man**    Just look to hit it then.
Keep aim.
And shoot.

**Boy**    I don't want to hurt it.

**Man**    You're shooting it.

**Boy**    Yeah but I don't want to just hurt it.

**Man**    Will you just . . .

*The* **Boy** *shoots.*

*The shot rings out.*

**Boy**    Did I get it?

**Man**    I don't . . .
I can't see it.

**Boy**    Did I hit it?

**Man**    I'll have a look.

*The* **Man** *exits to the bush.*

**Boy**    Did I hit it in the head?

*Pause.*

*The* **Man** *returns.*

**Man**    No.
You didn't get it.

**Boy**    I hit it.

**Man**    No, you didn't.

**Boy**    Didn't want to just hurt it.
Is it hurt?

**Man**    You didn't get it.

**Boy**    How do you know?

**Man**    Because it wouldn't have been able to run away.
One of these bullets.
It'd shatter the hips or the chest.
Wouldn't get away after that.

**Boy**    Are you sure?

**Man**    Course I'm sure.
I know what I'm doing.

*He takes the gun.*

Come on.
We'll find some more.

**Boy**    I don't want to shoot anymore.

**Man**    You don't have to.


**Nine**

*Later.*

*The bank of a small river.*

*They have two dead rabbits next to them.*

*The **Man** is washing his face in the river.*

*The **Boy** is looking at the dead rabbits.*

**Man**    Here.
Wash your hands.

**Boy**    Do they feel it?

**Man**    Yes.
But not for long.

*Beat.*

**Boy**    You're a good aim.

**Man**    It's just practice.
I used to do this a lot as a boy.
The rabbits are pests on the farm.
Used to get five pence for every one.
Come and wash your hands.
Yeah?

*The* **Boy** *joins the* **Man** *at the river.*

**Boy**    How many did you kill?

**Man**    I don't know.
Kept me up-to-date with football stickers though.
So enough.

*Beat.*

**Boy**    I'm not sure if I like it.

**Man**    That's OK. You've tried it.

*Silence.*

**Boy**    You should've taken the first shot.
That rabbit could be in agony now.
Not peaceful like these ones.

**Man**    You can't think like that.
Got to shut it out.

*Pause.*

**Boy**    Are we going to eat them?

**Man**    No.
We don't eat them.

**Boy**    Why not?

**Man**    Because we've got enough food.

*Beat.*

**Boy**    Then why did we kill them?

**Man**    For fun.

**Boy**    I don't know if it's fun.

**Man**    Because you're thinking too much
about the rabbits.

**Boy**    I can't help it.

**Man**    You'll get over it.
Don't worry.
It's like cigarettes.
You cough like hell with your first few.
But you get over it.
And once you get over it
you can start to enjoy it.

**Boy**    Smoking's bad for you.

**Man**    Well, yeah.

**Boy**    Don't you think?

**Man**    Yeah it is.
No, it's really bad for you.
Don't smoke.
I'm just saying.

*Pause.*

When I said we can do things differently.
I didn't just mean the washing up.
I mean talking too.
It's important you have a man you can talk to.
It's not the same with your mother.

**Boy**    I know.

**Man**    But if there's no one there then you can't know.
That's what I'm saying.

**Boy**    But I do know.
I talk to Mr Davies.

**Man**    Who's that?

**Boy**    He's my history teacher.

**Man**   That's not the same.

**Boy**   We talk about football.

**Man**   But it's not the same.

**Boy**   Why not?

**Man**   He's a teacher.

**Boy**   So?

**Man**   So he won't be honest with you.

**Boy**   He doesn't lie.

**Man**   I don't mean lying.
I mean . . .
He'll only tell you things he's allowed to.

**Boy**   Like what?

**Man**   Fuck. I don't know.
He'd tell you not to drink.

**Boy**   You drink too much.

**Man**   And you're too much like your fucking mother.

*Silence.*

I didn't mean that.

**Boy**   Yes, you did.

*Pause.*

**Man**   I just thought
if it rains
have you brought a cagoule?

**Boy**   Yes.
Have you?

**Man**   No. I forgot.
I don't need one though.

*Beat.*

**Boy**    You can borrow mine.

**Man**    I'll be alright.

*Pause.*

**Boy**    I stopped seeing Hannah
because she won't let me have sex with her.
She told me I was too pushy.
I called her a fucking boring bitch
and that I don't want to see her anymore.

**Man**    Christ.

*Pause.*

**Boy**    Why do you hate my mother?

**Man**    What makes you think I hate her?

**Boy**    Because you act as if you do.

**Man**    How?

**Boy**    By not talking to her.

**Man**    That's not hate.

**Boy**    Then what is it?

*Pause.*

**Man**    I don't know.
Confusion.

*Beat.*

**Boy**    When I get confused I ask for help.

*Silence.*

**Man**    I know you do.
That's good.

*The **Man** gets up. He picks up the corpses of the rabbits and throws them in the bushes.*

Come on.

**Ten**

*Night.*

*The camp.*

*The fire is lit.*

*They are both sat where the sky is open.*

*They are looking at the stars.*

**Man**   What's wrong?

**Boy**   We should've done something with the rabbits.

**Man**   What do you mean?

**Boy**   I don't know.

**Man**   Did you want to bury them?

**Boy**   No.

**Man**   Then what?

**Boy**   You should only hunt if you're going to eat it.

**Man**   I can't cook rabbits.

*Beat.*

You want a drink?

**Boy**   A coke.

*The **Man** gets up and grabs a coke and a beer out of the coolbox.*

**Man**   If we get some water.
From the river.
We put it in the box here.
It'll help keep it cooler.

*He sits back down and hands the **Boy** a can.*

**Boy**   Is that true?

**Man**   It'll help.

*Pause.*

You ever sleep outside?

**Boy**    No.

**Man**    I used to.

**Boy**    When you were young?

**Man**    Younger.

*Silence.*

**Boy**    I sometimes think I'm missing out.

**Man**    What do you mean?

**Boy**    You talk about so much I don't know.
I don't know how to shoot, to put up a tent.
I don't know what a fuck buddy is.

**Man**    You're young.
You'll learn.
We all learn things.
I'm still learning now.

**Boy**    Like what?

**Man**    Personal things.

**Boy**    Oh.

*Pause.*

**Man**    Are you happy?

**Boy**    I don't know.
I've got nothing to be unhappy about.

*Beat.*

**Man**    Do you ever get scared?

**Boy**    What of?

**Man**    Anything.

**Boy**   No.
   Well, yeah.
   But only the big things.

**Man**   The big things?

**Boy**   Global warming.
   Nuclear war.

**Man**   Right . . .

**Boy**   Why'd you say *right* like that?

**Man**   They're not real things.

**Boy**   They are real.
   If a bomb goes off it's real.

**Man**   But real right now.
   To you.

*Pause*.

   You know what happiness is?

**Boy**   No?

**Man**   Happiness is not having anything real to worry about.

*Beat*.

**Boy**   Like you?

**Man**   What?

**Boy**   You've got nothing to worry about, have you?
   You just dropped everything.
   Let Mum look after me, the house, everything.
   Is that what you were doing?
   Making it so you've got nothing
   to worry about anymore?

**Man**   It wasn't like that.

**Boy**   Yes, it was.

**Man**   You don't know how it is.

**Boy**    Seeing Mum crying every night.
Seeing her alone.
Whilst you're out with your fuck buddies.

**Man**    You don't know what a fuck buddy is.

*Pause.*

If you did you'd know I don't have any.

**Boy**    I know you've ruined my family.

*Beat.*

**Man**    I'm sorry.

*Pause.*

I said I'm sorry.

**Boy**    OK.

**Man**    But your mother's poisoning your mind.
You don't know me.

**Boy**    You kill rabbits for no reason.

**Man**    I said I can't cook them.
I explained.
I'm sorry.


**Eleven**

*The next morning.*

*The camp.*

*Breakfast.*

*They are sat at opposite ends of the fire, which is now just hot embers.*

*They are eating in silence.*

**Boy**    I want to go shooting today.

**Man**    No.

**Boy**    What?

**Man**    We're not shooting today.

**Boy**    But I want to.

*Pause.*

**Man**    You're too angry.
  Just be wasting bullets.

**Boy**    You think I'm a rubbish shot.

**Man**    That's not it.

**Boy**    I need to practice.

**Man**    You're angry.
  You won't be able to concentrate.
  Look.
  You're practically shaking.

**Boy**    It's these beans.
  They're too fucking hot.

**Man**    Hey.
  You watch your language.

**Boy**    Fuck you.

**Man**    Fuck me?
  Fuck you you little cunt.
  Who do you think you are?
  I'm your fucking dad
  you little . . .

*The **Man** throws his plate of food across the camp.*

*Pause.*

  Shit.

*The **Man** goes and picks up the plate.*

*He calms himself.*

  We're going fishing today.
  You ever been fishing?

*He triest to pick up bits of the fallen food.*

**Boy**    No.

**Man**    No.
So we'll do that.
It'll be good for fishing.
I said that river'll be good for fishing.
Good day for it.

*Pause.*

I'll pack our stuff, then.

*He gets up and goes to the tent.*

**Boy**    I think I hate you.

*He stops.*

**Man**    That's OK.

*He continues packing the bag.*


**Twelve**

*Later that day.*

*At the river.*

*They are sat with the fishing rod on a stand.*

*The **Man** is drinking a beer.*

*The **Boy** is eating a sandwich.*

*The **Boy** stops eating.*

**Man**    You alright?

**Boy**    Yeah.

**Man**    We can leave the rod.
Don't worry.
It'll just rest there.

*Pause.*

What's wrong with the sandwich?

**Boy**   Nothing.
Just not hungry.

*Beat.*

**Man**   Don't you like fishing?

**Boy**   We're not doing anything.

**Man**   That's the point.
Fishing is a hunt.
Just like with the gun.
Except it's about luring.
Tricking the fish.

**Boy**   By not doing anything?

**Man**   By not attacking it.
Nature is about pounce and attack and surprise.
That's what the fish look out for.
We're cleverer than the fish.
So we adapt ourselves.

*Pause.*

**Boy**   Then why haven't we caught anything?

**Man**   Because it isn't as simple as that.
It's about the conditions too.

**Boy**   Are these good conditions?

**Man**   They're OK.
People who don't fish
seem to think that raining
is the best weather for fishing.
You know, for river fishing
a good rain season helps
because it swells the river
and encourages fresh fish to run in from the sea.
But for some reason you don't catch many fish

when the river's at its highest.
You have to catch it at the right time
so when the water begins to clear.

**Boy**    You mean on its way back down?

**Man**    Yeah.
Yeah, that's it.

*Pause.*

**Boy**    What about this?
Is this at a good level?

**Man**    Well, we've had a lot of heavy rain
in the past few weeks.
This is still a little high.

**Boy**    Oh.

**Man**    But it's not just about the level of the river.
You need to be on the lookout
for the most delicate of changes in the atmosphere.
Because that can affect the readiness
of the fish to come out too.
A glimpse of sunshine on a dull day.
A rise in pressure.
Drop in the wind.
Change in temperature or something.
But really, all you can do, is just be there.
You know, you can only catch fish if you're at the river.
Some people, they're all in for the fancy equipment.
Expensive rods. Nets.
Studying readings of the levels of rivers.
All this pretentious stuff.
But if you've got all that
and you don't trust the fish or yourself
then you'll never catch anything.
Sometimes you've just got to ignore that.
And be there.
That's what I do.
I'm a very instinctive fisher.

**Boy**    Do you catch much?

**Man**    Not really.
We've got no bait
so we're having to use bits of sausage from breakfast.
Maybe they don't like sausage.

*The **Boy** starts laughing.*

What are you laughing at?
What . . . what is it?

*The **Boy**'s laughing causes the **Man** to start laughing.*

*The laughing dies down.*

*Silence.*

**Boy**    Why did you not say anything
when I said I thought I hated you?

**Man**    Because you need someone to blame.
You need to be able to focus all that on something.
    Someone.
I get that.

*Pause.*

**Boy**    Don't you care that I hate you?

**Man**    Of course I do.

**Boy**    Then why aren't you trying to change it?

**Man**    I am.

**Boy**    How?

**Man**    By just letting you do it.
Letting you say it.
Working it out.

*Beat.*

I'm not going to keep asking you questions
about how you feel.

You don't have to justify yourself to me.
It's ok to just feel things.
Things with no logic.
Things that are unfair.

*Pause.*

It's thinking about you that . . .
I once went back to the lake.
After your mum.
I went back there and it dawned on me.
Yeah.
It's you, it is.

*Pause.*

**Boy**   What?

**Man**    Nothing.
I don't know.
I'm sorry I shouted at you before.

**Boy**   It's OK.
I'm sorry I was rude to you.


**Thirteen**

*Later.*

*They are walking back to camp.*

*The **Boy** stops, the **Man** doesn't notice and continues walking.*

**Boy**   Hang on.

**Man**   What?
We need to get back.

**Boy**   This is where we were yesterday.

**Man**   That's it, mate.
It's good you're recognising.

**Boy**   It was around here we started shooting.

**Man**   Yeah.

**Boy**   A straight line from the camp.

**Man**   Yeah.
   Now you're getting it.

**Boy**   And we stopped here.

**Man**   About here, yeah.

**Boy**   And I shot.

**Man**   And you shot.

**Boy**   Then is that the rabbit?

**Man**   What?

**Boy**   That.
   Is that my rabbit?

*The* **Boy** *walks to the bush.*

**Man**   Hang on.
   I said hang on.
   Don't just walk off.

**Boy**   You said I didn't hit it.
   You said if it could run away
   it means I didn't hit it.

**Man**   I know I did.

**Boy**   But I did hit it.
   And it could run away.

**Man**   It might not be the same rabbit.

**Boy**   Course it is.

**Man**   Yeah.

*Beat.*

**Boy**   Did you know I hit it?

*Beat.*

**Man**    Yeah.

**Boy**    You it hid under the bush.

**Man**    I kicked it under the bush.
So you didn't have to see it.

**Boy**    Why did you tell me I didn't hit it?

**Man**    Because you said you didn't want to just hurt it.

**Boy**    But I did.

**Man**    Yeah.

**Boy**    Why didn't you tell me?

**Man**    Because I didn't want you to feel bad.

*Pause.*

**Boy**    I do feel bad.

**Man**    Yeah.

**Boy**    I feel sick.

**Man**    You'll be alright.

*Pause.*

**Boy**    I don't want to leave it.

**Man**    We can't take it.

**Boy**    Why not?

**Man**    What can we do with it?

**Boy**    Eat it.

**Man**    I can't cook rabbit.

**Boy**    But we killed it.

**Man**    Yeah, but not to eat.

**Boy**    Please.

**Man**    I don't know.
I don't know how to do it.

**Boy**    Please.

**Man**    It's getting late.
We should be walking.

*The* **Man** *goes to leave.*

*The* **Boy** *doesn't move.*

**Boy**    Do you know what you want?

**Man**    What do you mean?
Like now?
I want a warm fire now.
Some food.
Those paper sausages are sounding quite good.

**Boy**    No.
I mean in life.

*Pause.*

**Man**    What are you on about?

**Boy**    Don't know.

**Man**    It's a strange question to ask.

**Boy**    Is it?

**Man**    Yeah.

**Boy**    Why?

**Man**    What made you think to ask me?

**Boy**    My mum asks me.

**Man**    Well, that's probably because she doesn't understand what you're going through.

**Boy**    No.
She asks me about you.

*Pause.*

**Man**    Well, I don't know.
I don't know myself.

**Boy**    I wish she'd stop asking me.

**Man**    I'm sorry.

**Boy**    I don't understand why you're unhappy.

*Beat.*

**Man**    That's OK.

**Boy**    Stop saying it's OK.
It's not OK.
You've got nothing to be unhappy about.
You should be happy.

**Man**    It doesn't work like that.

**Boy**    Well, it should.

**Man**    What about not having anything to make you happy?

**Boy**    But you have us.

**Man**    I have you.
But that's not the same.
I can't live my life through you.

**Boy**    I wish you'd come home.

**Man**    It's not my home anymore.
It hasn't been for a long time.

**Boy**    I think you're being very selfish.

*Pause.*

**Man**    I know.
I know.
Come on.

*The **Man** picks up the rabbit.*

You carry the gun.
I'll take this.

**Boy**    We're taking it?

**Man**    Yeah.
Before it's dark.
Come on.


**Fourteen**

*Dusk.*

*The camp.*

*The* **Man** *has the rabbit and a knife.*

**Boy**    What are you going to do?

**Man**    I don't know.
I suppose I just cut it.

**Boy**    Where do you cut it?

**Man**    I don't know.
The end.

**Boy**    Which end?

**Man**    I don't think it matters.

**Boy**    Are you sure it's dead?

**Man**    Of course it's fucking dead.
No, look.
Sorry.
Just sit over there.
Let me do this.

*The* **Boy** *sits down.*

*The* **Man** *goes to cut it, but hesitates.*

*He sinks the knife in the side of the rabbit.*

*He panics at the blood and drops it.*

*He picks it back up, his hands shaking.*

Right.
Oh.

**Boy**   Ah, dad.

**Man**   It's alright.
It's going to bleed.

*He tries to cut it to skin again but hacks away at it.*

**Boy**   Dad, no.

**Man**   Maybe don't watch.
Go over there.

**Boy**   Dad, watch what you're /

*Innards fall out of it.*

**Man**   Ah, fuck.
Ah, it's alright.
That bit's meant to fall out.

**Boy**   Is it?

**Man**   Well, it doesn't look eatable.

**Boy**   None of it does.

**Man**   Well, not like this.
Not when I've got my hand up it.
Not when it's covered in fucking blood.

*He throws the rabbit down and drops the knife.*

I'm sorry.
I can't . . .
I can't do it.

**Boy**   Dad, I'm sorry.

**Man**   I can't cook rabbits.

**Boy**   I don't want you to.

**Man**   It just fell apart.

**Boy**   I didn't mean this.

**Man**   You wanted me to skin a rabbit.
 What did you think was going to happen?

*The* **Man** *gets up.*

 I'm going to clean up.


**Fifteen**

*Night.*

*The river.*

*The* **Man** *is sat, washing his hands.*

*The* **Boy** *enters.*

**Boy**   You left me.
 You left me alone in the camp.
 You just walked off and it was getting dark.

**Man**   I had to wash my hands.
 You know the river.

**Boy**   Could've got lost.

**Man**   No, I couldn't.

**Boy**   I could've.

*Beat.*

**Man**   You hate me.

**Boy**   No, I don't.

**Man**   You said you do.

*Beat.*

 Your mother asked me to leave.
 When we split up.
 I didn't walk out.
 She asked me to go.

*Beat.*

You might hate me but I went for you.
For her.
For me too.
I mean, fuck, I can think about me, can't I?

**Boy**    Is that what it is?
You thinking about yourself?

**Man**    A little bit.

**Boy**    You left to come out here?

**Man**    Not out here, no.
But a little bit.
And it's enough.

**Boy**    Is it?

**Man**    Yeah.
Might not seem that much to you.
That's alright.
We can't all have everything we want.

**Boy**    Right.

**Man**    What?

**Boy**    That's your advice to me, is it?

**Man**    Well it's true.
You need to understand that it is ok
to be unhappy with your life.
To not have any goals or aims.
These things are not as essential
as they are made out to be.
The world won't check you
to make sure you've done enough with your life.
It is very easy to underachieve.
When my dad took me out camping like this.
This is the kind of thing he should have said to me.

*Pause.*

**Boy**    Do you regret having me?

**Man**    Yeah.

*Beat.*

I'm sorry.

*Silence.*

**Boy**    Why did you say that?

**Man**    Because I love you.
And I'm going to be honest with you.
And I'm honestly telling you that
I'm a failure and I love you.

*Beat.*

The rabbits will still come out.
Not expecting to ever get shot at
but they always do.
And they're never prepared for it.
But maybe some of them are.
And maybe those that are don't die.
I know disappointment.
I'm a rabbit that's been shot at enough times
to recognise that.

*Silence.*

After your mother and I split up.
What I was telling you before
I went back to the farm and the lake.
And it's not as fresh or crisp anymore.
And it is swampy and cold.
And I stood there.
And I made a decision.
And I tell you
you only need to make that decision
once in your life
for it to stay with you.
I dived in.
I dived in and I tried to drown.

But I couldn't.
I just kept rising to the top.
I couldn't even do that.
Got out on the rocks and sat there.
The only thing that came to me was you.
What I have to be to you.

*Silence.*

I was there and I made that decision.

*Pause.*

We should be getting back.

**Boy**   It's dark.

**Man**   Yeah.

**Boy**   We could stay out here.
Like you said you used to.

**Man**   Yeah.
If you're alright with that?

**Boy**   Yeah.

*Pause.*

**Man**   Are you warm enough?

**Boy**   Yeah. I am.

**Man**   You sure?

**Boy**   Dad.

**Man**   Sorry.

*Beat.*

**Boy**   Dad?

**Man**   Yeah?

**Boy**   Are you alright now?

**Man**    Yes, son.
Yes, I'm alright now.


**Sixteen**

*The next morning.*

*The camp.*

*They are packing their things.*

*The tent is down. The fire is out.*

**Man**    It's alright.
If you roll the sleeping bags
I'll do the tent.

*Pause.*

**Boy**    What did Granddad do whilst you put the tent up?

**Man**    What?

**Boy**    If putting the tent up was your job
what did he do?

**Man**    He smoked his pipe.

**Boy**    Why don't you leave it to me?

**Man**    Because when I was your age I wanted to be taught.
It's as not as much fun on your own.

*Pause.*

**Boy**    What if I want to come with you?

**Man**    Where?

**Boy**    Home.
Your home.

**Man**    And stay with me?

**Boy**    Yeah.

**Man**  You don't want to stay with me.

**Boy**  Why not?

**Man**  I don't think it would work.

**Boy**  You don't know that.

*Pause.*

**Man**  Your mother needs you.

**Boy**  So do you.

**Man**  Will you pass me that bag?

**Boy**  Will you tell Mum how you feel?

**Man**  It's not her worry.

**Boy**  I can tell her for you.

**Man**  Please.
Let's just get this done.

*Pause.*

**Boy**  I want you to be happy.

**Man**  We had a good time, didn't we?
We can do this.
More of this.
But something too regular you'd get bored of.
We can't let this to get boring.

**Boy**  I don't know if that's how it works.

**Man**  You wouldn't know.

**Boy**  Neither would you.

*Beat.*

**Man**  Let's get this done.

**Boy**  Who are you to tell me that life is shit
and then abandon me in it?

**Man**   I'm your father.
   No one else will tell you.
   No one else is responsible.

**Boy**   You keep saying *responsible*
   but you're not being responsible at all.

**Man**   I'm doing my best.

**Boy**   I want to live with you.

**Man**   No, you want me and your mother back together
   and that's not going to happen.
   You want everything as it was
   but that's not going to happen.
   Things change.
   People move on.
   I'm not your mother's husband.

**Boy**   But you're still my dad.

**Man**   Yeah and I can be your dad.
   You certainly need one.
   You need to learn to put up a tent.
   Ask a girl out properly.
   Fuck, you need to learn to ask a girl out properly.
   Things your mother can't give you.
   She may be there for the big stuff.
   The important stuff.
   Well, that's good. I'm glad she is.
   But sometimes you're going to need
   something else.
   Something you can relate to when you fuck up.

*The* **Man** *sits down.*

*Beat.*

*The* **Boy** *sits down by him.*

   You tell your mother this
   she's not going to let you come again.

**Boy**    I won't tell her.

**Man**    Then what are you going to say?

**Boy**    I'll say we shot rabbits.

*End.*

# Even Stillness Breathes Softly Against a Brick Wall

'To be modern is to find ourselves in an environment that promises us adventure, power, joy, growth, transformation of ourselves and the world – and at the same time that threatens to destroy everything we have, everything we know, everything we are.'

Marshall Berman, *All That Is Solid Melts into Air*

'Meanwhile everyone wants to breathe and nobody can breathe and many say "we will breathe later". And most of them don't die because they are already dead.'

Raoul Vaneigem, *The Revolution of Everyday Life*

## Characters

**Him**
**Her**

## Design

*Spaces within a small flat.*

*Fractions of furniture and props to indicate where in the flat we are, for example, a bath indicates the bathroom, and so on.*

## Sound

*Cold, electronic, minimalist.*

*During Act Three, a constant low hum at just under 20 Hz (no lower than 17 Hz) – just below threshold of human audibility – to create a state of disorientation and unease in the audience.*

## Act One

**One**

*They appear.*

**Him**  Wake up.

**Her**  Wake up.

**Him**  Every morning I wake before her.
But I don't get up till she does.

**Her**  I have to make the tea
otherwise he'd be in bed all day.

The kitchen floor is cold on my feet.
No matter how close to the bed I leave my slippers
I always step over and forget them in the morning.

**Him**  As I get up I trip over her slippers.

**Her**  Maybe I should sleep with them in my arms.
Then I won't forget.
But would the hard plastic soles
prove more uncomfortable in the night
than the cold kitchen floor in the morning?

**Him**  As soon as I'm up I'm bursting for a piss.

**Her**  While the kettle boils and the sound of him pissing
echoes through the hall
I wake myself up.

**Him**  How I haven't pissed myself in the night
is a marvel and testament to the proficiency
of the human body.

**Her**  I rattle through a plan for the day in my head.
Even though I don't want to, I can't help it.

**Him**   I catch sight of myself in the mirror.
My legs and arms and cock and chest
underwhelm me.

**Her**   I take the tea to the bedroom
and he's already in the shower
and halfway through the first verse
of 'Want You Back'.

**Him** (*sings*)   'But someone picked you from the bunch
One glance was all it took
Now it's much too late for me
To take a second look.
Oh baby give me one more chance . . . '

**Her**   I iron whatever bits I'd planned to do last night
but didn't bother with.

**Him**   I pride myself on only ever having to take
ten minutes in the shower.

**Her**   After twenty minutes he gets out.
The bathroom is wet and warm like breath.

**Him**   I sip the tea she made me and get dressed.

**Her**   The first words we say to each other
are often just slight variations
on the theme of how late we are.

**Him**   We get to the bus stop and have a bit of a faff
about whether or not she's remembered
half her handbag.

**Her**   The heaving bus lurches towards us.
Busy with the commuting and the mad
bunched together.

**Him**   A shipment to the city.
Bussed in and bussed out
stopping everywhere that doesn't matter
where the don't care and don't mind get off.
We sneer at everyone else's stops.

**Her**   I touch up my eye-liner.
And try not to catch the eye of the old man
sat behind me
in my compact mirror.

**Him**   I get off after her and head to the office.
I won't be late but
for the sake of being a worrying fucker
I panic as if I will be.

**Her**   As I get to my desk
I see I've already got three voicemail messages.
It is not yet nine o'clock and I feel a martyr
for doing anything before the day officially starts.

**Him**   I see Mr Collins and speculate on whether
he ever actually leaves the office.
Spending his nights upstairs laying more eggs
mothering them into hatching.
A fresh new batch of worker drones.

**Her**   I go to take the messages but I find them to be
just cold calls automated.
Empty and echoey. Tin and dead.
Recorded from another space and time.
The computers that programmed these messages
have no idea what their purpose is.
They don't know their pulses
are meant for human ears.
But if they did I wonder what they'd rather say.

**Him**   I'm as bland as my tie and as straight
as the crease down the front of my trousers.
My degree in Business Studies did not prepare me
for being this inconsequential.
I dress to look a cheap deal for my boss.
But it's what you do.
It's what you are.
In this economy it's the way you have to be.

**Her**    I have a shirt that blends
with every coat of paint in the building.

**Him**    I walk past reception and imagine the girls there
talking about me.
I'm friends with neither of them on Facebook
but I have three mutual friends with one
and five mutual friends with the other.

**Her**    The morning passes and I do nothing
but take calls and forward them on.
I type up the odd letter and open the post.

**Him**    I am a still-life portrait waiting to be painted.
My work is dull but I'm not complaining.
Don't think that I'm fucking complaining.

**Her**    My day is defined by my breaks
and the only true measure of progress I have
is how many times I wash up my cup.

**Him**    One of the interns makes me a cup of tea
and I say thank you.
I sympathise with the interns
and the shit they wade through.

**Her**    There's no moment in the day
not one symbolic or literal event
that assures me my work here is worthwhile.
But it is a safe job.
And safety outweighs satisfaction
and my government agrees.

**Him**    But when I was an intern
I fucking hated the people in my position.
I stop myself from sipping the tea he made me.

**Her**    The men in the office start talking about football.
And as I don't want to sound like a vinegar tits
I disguise my hatred of their banter.

**Him**   I'd have spat in my tea if I was him.
I'd have spat in it and called me a cunt.
Am I a cunt?

**Her**   I'm only ever brought into the conversation
when they want to ironically or otherwise
compare themselves to a girl.

**Him**   Does he look me in the eye and call me a cunt?

**Her**   Course I'd never imagine saying anything.
I'm a woman of childbearing age.
Am I hell going to cause a fuss.
Don't think that I'm fucking complaining.

**Him**   Should I invite them to five-a-side?
Should I make them my mates?

**Her**   You get on with it and you manage yourself.
I conduct myself in a way
my mother doesn't have to.

**Him**   I wonder what Dave would say
about me bringing all these fuckers to football.

**Her**   You work the woman out of you.

**Him**   They'd bump up the numbers I suppose.
And maybe one of them
would have a decent left foot.

**Her**   You are all potential boys.

**Him**   I spend the rest of the day
anticipating all the interns calling me a cunt
under their breath
by calling them 'mate'
as soon as we make eye contact.

**Her**   You will get along.
You will be easy to work with.

**Him**   I wonder if Mr Collins worries
about people thinking he's a cunt.

Probably not.
He probably thrives on it.
I need to thrive on it.

**Her**   The afternoon drags like the morning
except outside starts to shift to a slow fade.
And people are now yawning
because they've been up too long
rather than yawning
because they've not slept enough.

**Him**   I chew my way through the afternoon.

**Her**   I make it through another day
by not being too much
and by being just enough.

**Him**   Home time.

**Her**   We cling to our burdens with white knuckles.
I cannot be relieved of this position.
I am worth my wages and my cost to the company.

**Him**   I pick her up from her work
and we drift through the usual small talk
of office politics and minor news stories
that have littered our days.

**Her**   A cat watches us get off the bus back at home.
Her eyes are the colour of amber traffic lights.
And I know it's a she because all cats are girls.

**Him**   We rely on the idea that we're both fighting.
We go through it because we must.
And because we must we pretend to care.

**Her**   The bus is just a box that
sends us from one place to another.

**Him**   I care about her but I don't care about her work.
In the same way one veteran won't care
about another veteran's war.
Too close. Too raw.

**Her**    We have no choice in the direction of the box
and I wonder if it can take us to any place
we don't already go.

**Him**    We get home and in some ways that's enough.

**Her**    That's enough.

*End of One.*

### Two

**He** *appears and turns on the lights, the television, his laptop, his iPod in its dock, the kettle, and starts playing with his phone before he takes off his jacket and tie.*

*The house-phone rings.* **He** *picks it up. His mobile rings.* **He** *picks it up.*

*An email comes through to his laptop.*

**He** *exits and returns with a supermarket pre-packaged sandwich.* **He** *opens the box, lays it out on the table and, to the theme of his orchestra of electronic goods, starts to eat his sandwich.*

**She** *appears having come home from work.* **She** *takes off her coat and puts her bag down and exits.*

**She** *returns with her own sandwich and sits next to him.* **He** *finishes his sandwich and exits as* **She** *starts eating hers.*

*End of Two.*

### Three

**He** *appears.*

**Him**    The air conditioner in the office won't work
and while it is neither warm nor my job
I am asked to have a look at it.

**She** *continues eating her sandwich.*

**Him**   I see nothing but a broken machine.
I'm no mechanic but things don't half work.
They're either working or they're not.
I waste my time.

I spend a good ten minutes with it.
I tell them that it doesn't appear
to be able to switch on.
They ask if I know how to fix it and I say no.
They sigh and tell me they're going to have to call
someone proper out.
And they linger on the word 'proper'
as if it was my idea to have a look at it.
Like I give a shit.
Like I give half a fucking shit.
Am I not proper to you?

**He** *watches* **Her** *for a moment.*

**Him**   I get back to my desk and I've missed a call.
I check the number and it's my parents.
I wonder why my mum would be calling.

I don't ring her back as I have a whole afternoon
planned for doing much more important things
like looking at Winona Ryder's Wikipedia page.
I find celebrities enormously attractive.

**He** *disappears.*

**Her**   The cardboard packaging on my Tesco sandwich
is not too dissimilar from the bread.
I know it's not the healthiest thing in the world
but it's the easiest thing in the world.
I am not a woodland creature.
I will not eat seeds and berries.
*Heat* magazine does not fuel me.
The lifestyle section of the *Guardian*
does not feed me.
These grey processed foods may be empty
but they are predictable and satisfying.

The plastic highs of MSG
and echoing carbohydrates.
You know where you are with a pre-packed meal.
A thousand will taste the same
and there's security in that.
Snack packs. Bio fuels. Meal for one.

*End of Three.*


**Four**

**He** *appears.*

**Him**    I get a text from my dad saying he called the office
and did I get his message.
I ring him
and ask what he's doing home on a Monday.
He tells me he has nowhere else to be.

There's a point in your life when you realise
that your parents are just people too.
That they're not betters or elders
they're just equals.
And sometimes not even that.

They made him redundant on Friday
and it was only on Monday morning
when he got up with the alarm
that it hit him.
He is not required to be up on a Monday morning.
He's not required to be up on any morning.

Weighed up and evaluated
my dad found himself not cost effective.
A piece of paper. A calculator.
His livelihood.
That's the fucking economy.

I ask him how mum took the news
and he tells me he'll let me know
once he's found a way of telling her.

*End of Four.*


**Five**

*They appear.*

**Him**    Wake up.

**Her**    Wake up.

**Him**    I had a dream that we were on the bus
and on the way to work.
The traffic was moving so fast and
the bus wouldn't slow down
because there were so many other cars behind it.

But then something happened
and all the cars started crashing.
But as they crashed the cars didn't stop moving
and the cars were getting more and more mangled.
Like a wave of destroyed cars.
I woke up as the bus folded in on us.

**Her**    Are you getting up yet?

**Him**    We get ready and leave.

**Her**    The cat didn't watch us leave
and I'm disappointed.
But it will be there tonight.

**Him**    The same colours of windowed tins
on bitumen skin.
The heat of other cars cooks through our seats.

**Her**    I irrationally think the cat only comes out
to watch us.
And that it comes to show us

that we're not just people,
we're not just someone else.
We're us and in some ways
our us is greater than other people's.

**Him**    We all pour into the city like water down a sink.
Fucking plughole city.
I used to think my dad knew
how the world worked.
I see my office and I see the type
that would be first against the wall.
And the idea of my dad as one of them
is a bit fucking embarrassing.

**Her**    There's something burning inside of him.

**Him**    I don't work because I want to.
I don't make myself essential to the company
because I fucking want to.

**Her**    I know I'll worry about him all day.
He might not have said anything
but the quiet types never do
and his eyes scream stress
and I know how much he can cope with.

**Him**    The rest of the world thinks my dad is pointless.
If my parents can't cope then what chance
have I got?

**Her**    I get an email calling me upstairs.
Maybe they figured they could sack me
and not miss me.
I will not miss the company either.

**Him**    I go to make a cup of tea to get away from my desk.

**Her**    As I walk to the lift I'm aware of Chris and Tom
and Peter and Harry at their desks.
I feel them watch me.
And I get a tense feeling just above my vagina.

**Him**   You don't have to do too much in this world.
You just have to work and earn your way.

**Her**   I don't turn back to them when I'm in the lift.
I don't acknowledge the stares
and I let the feeling pass.
I am not a flirt.

**Him**   The old bastard Frank creeps behind me
and makes me jump in the kitchen.
I drop a cup and it smashes on the floor.
The sound and the look of it
cracking and bouncing and bursting
makes me feel strangely good.
Frank just smiles and takes some biscuits
from the cupboard and leaves.
I have to stop myself from dropping another cup.

**Her**   In my boss's eyes I see
he thinks of himself as my Christ.
I cross my legs and hold my stomach.
I expect him to fire me.
I can feel him swallowing gulps of powerful air.
I can feel his erection in the room.

He offers me a promotion.
I ask doing what and he tells me
it's exactly the same job but on a different floor.
I am being asked to ignore
the corpses of the redundant.
I will be sat among their ghosts.
I don't refuse because I can't refuse.

**Him**   I hear something on the news
on how the forces in some fucking-istan
are storming their government buildings.
I imagine taking a bayonet upstairs
and performing a mild act of genocide
on Collins and his cronies.

**Her**    We are doing what we can
for ourselves and for each other.

I say thank you and he kisses me on the lips.

**Him**    I see an interview with a local man
caught up in the fighting.
I wonder what people care about in a war zone.
I wonder in what ways their problems change.
Yes you're fighting for your life
but what about your bills?
How do you feel about your relationship?

**Her**    I ascend into another level of commitment
to a job I only took
because there was nothing else out there.

**Him**    I pick her up from work and that's the day.

**Her**    That's the day.

*End of Five.*


### Six

**He** *appears.*

**He** *is watching the television as it yawns out decibels of colour.*

**He** *switches it off and goes to leave the room.*

*As* **He** *leaves, the television switches itself back on again.*

**He** *goes to the television, switches it off, goes to leave and again it switches itself back on.*

**He** *turns it off but as quickly as* **He** *does it turns back on. Again.*

*This time* **He** *doesn't turn it off.* **He** *just sits back down on the sofa.*

**She** *appears and sits down next to him and they watch together. End of Six.*

**Seven**

*They appear.*

*The television is on between them, spewing out white noise and a blizzard of 'snow'*

**Her**   Chloe texts me
telling me she's looking forward to New Year.
I presume she means the party
and not the empty promise of change
heralded by a new calendar year.
I text back saying so am I.

**Him**   Most evenings are in front of the television.
There is not the pressure to have your own opinions.
You are presented other people's dreams wholesale.

**Her**   I feel him radiating a stress he doesn't normally carry.

**Him**   We watch the small Middle Eastern state
getting spanked by missiles.
The ruins look like a map from *Call of Duty*.

**Her**   I haven't told him about the promotion.
My money doesn't change
and therefore the significance of my work
does not change.

**Him**   This could never happen to us.
We do things properly here.
We have a world that can't be bombed or battered.
We've finished with that.
We're dead to change.

**Her**   It's not that I want to keep it away from him.
I just can't see him being that bothered.

**Him**   There's a man on the television
holding the corpse of his son
and in the background there is music.

**Her**   And maybe there's a part of me
          that doesn't care what he thinks about it either.

**Him**   The most exciting thing I can do in that office
          is break the odd cup here and there.

**Her**   I hate myself for thinking that.

**Him**   There's a security in knowing
          a bomb will never fly out of the sky.
          We don't have to look up any more.

**Her**   We call these things progress.
          But progress to what?
          And to where?
          Where are we actually fucking going?

**Him**   We can just look forward and that's a good thing.
          And life might be hard but fuck.
          Tell these kids that are being bombed
          that life is fucking hard.

**Her**   He just sits watching the fighting and nothing else.

*End of Seven.*


**Eight**

**She** *appears.*

**Her**   Sometimes I wonder whether or not
          this is a relationship or just a default setting.

          And we're working
          we're working fucking hard
          for this imaginary goal of being happy together
          and in a kind of peace.
          But what is that kind of peace?
          What does it look like?
          Perhaps some things we're not meant to know.
          And the whys and the because of whats come later.

I have faith in him and that's all I need.
I hope that it's all I need.

*End of Eight.*


**Nine**

*They appear.*

**He** *is in front of the television. It oozes at him.*

**Her**    Dead to the world he watches the news.

**Him**    Between pieces on the conflict
they show a dog who acts like a person
and its owners treat it like a little boy.
And as ground troops are deployed
we vote for our favourite adverts.

**Her**    I spoke to your mum.

**Him**    She didn't tell me she was going to ring.

**Her**    I don't tell him it was me who called her.

**Him**    What did she say?

**Her**    She was surprised to hear
you didn't tell me about your dad.

**Him**    He didn't want people to know.

**Her**    It's nothing to be ashamed of.

**Him**    Imagine if I weren't working.

**Her**    We'd cope.

**Him**    I've had to lend them money.

**Her**    It's what we're there for.
It's what you do.

**Him**    She asks me why I kept it from her.

**Her**   We can manage.
I don't have to be involved
if you don't want me to be.

**Him**   I ask her how she can say that.
I couldn't do it without you.

**Her**   He breaks my heart without trying.
It is the softest tissue because I love him.

**Him**   Every decision I make is with you at its fucking heart.

**Her**   I wonder at what point
do we include time for ourselves.

**Him**   I tell her I only want to do what's best.

**Her**   I don't think what we are doing is what's best.

**Him**   I tell her I know.
I need you.

**Her**   And I know he does.
And maybe I haven't been there enough.
Maybe I've been letting him down too.

**Him**   I love you.

**Her**   And that is it.
Whatever challenges or problems we have
we love each other.
There's nothing else in the world except us.

**Him**   We watch the news.
The bombing has reached the rural provinces
and civil war has broken out.

*End of Act One.*

## Act Two

### One

**He** *appears.*

**He** *slowly gets dressed from one suit to another identical suit as the war blares at him from a television screen.*

**He** *takes time, he makes himself up slowly.*

**He** *is ready for work. End of One.*

### Two

*They appear.*

**Her**    Wake up.

**Him**    Wake up.

**Her**    Kettle on.
TV on.
Everything on.
The day is alive with electric hum.

**Him**    Morning news blaring.
The slow tense of every muscle begins again.

**Her**    People are already on Twitter.
Hashtag breakfast.

**Him**    Gulped my tea down without really noticing.
The cup still hot to touch.

**Her**    I shower.
The warm water runs down my hair
my body and my face.

**Him**    I wonder why someone so good
and so fucking beautiful has to work.

**Her**   I choose carefully what to wear.
   Which grey to put with which black.

**Him**   The dread builds about another day
   pushing my mind to keep going.
   Why am I doing this?
   Are we not here to expand as a species?

**Her**   We know the world will not change for us.
   But if we deal with it together
   and in tune with each other
   then we will be stronger than that.

   I put on my make-up.

**Him**   We leave.

**Her**   I take the backed-up post out of the little grey slot.
   If it wasn't for me he would let them pile up.

**Him**   She tuts but that's all it is.
   A tut.
   There's more to life than remembering the post.

**Her**   The cat watches us still and
   I'm now certain she's watching us
   out of sadness rather than fascination.
   I read too much into these things.

**Him**   Traffic.
   Car cholesterol.
   The same every day.

**Her**   I don't like to think that the cat watches us
   because it knows something terrible.
   I'd rather it watched everyone if that's the case.

**Him**   A young girl on a bike screams
   at the bus as it cuts her up.
   'Watch where you're fucking going,'
   and through the window she looks at me.

**Her**    I realise I don't have any cash for lunch.
  I don't mind paying on my card
  but you feel a bit of twat
  paying on a card with the meal deal.

**Him**    And I think, well, it's not my fucking fault.
  Why did she look at me
  when I was just fucking sat there?
  Look at your fucking self.
  And I wish the driver had ploughed into the cunt.

**Her**    But then I think fuck it.
  Money is money and they'll take it
  however fucking way I give it to them.

**Him**    When I get to work I read an article online
  about how tomorrow's global war will be nuclear
  and last just minutes.
  The thought haunts me all day.

**Her**    I peel the stamps off envelopes and save them.

**Him**    Thanks to the television
  the radio and the internet by ten a.m.
  I have encountered international misery
  and actual human suffering
  more times than I have encountered
  any kind of personal satisfaction.

**Her**    I never use the stamps I save.
  I let them build up in my drawer.
  I never think to question my routine.

**Him**    My computer crashes
  and takes all my progress and work with it.
  I feel myself breathing in particles
  of disconnected wi-fi.

**Her**    That's a lie.
  I question what I do
  every single moment of the day.

**Him**   The computer splutters back to life
and a backlog of emails flood through.
One hour ago. Two hours ago. Three hours ago.
Urgent. Priority. Urgent.

**Her**   I type up a letter.

**Him**   I panic. My fingers shake as I reply.
Apologise. Explain. Rinse. Repeat.
See email from Collins. Fuck.
Don't even want to open it.

**Her**   I answer the twenty-fourth call of the day.

**Him**   I have a cup of coffee for lunch.

**Her**   The man on the other end doesn't want to talk
he wants to shout.
I do not know who he is
though he believes himself justified
in calling me a cunt.
I hang up and tell my boss about the abuse.
Though he is more concerned
that I hung up the phone.
It is company policy to never hang up the phone.

**Him**   The computer crashes again
just as I'm preparing for another meeting.

**Her**   The phone rings and I dread picking it up.

**Him**   I receive nothing but jeers from my colleagues.
Half sniffing an opportunity to take advantage
of my misfortune
half not understanding
how to honestly convey empathy.

**Her**   After a few moments
of weighing up whether or not
not answering the phone now would manifest itself
in not answering the phone ever again
I bite the bullet and prepare myself

to be called a cunt for the second time.
I pick up the phone and it is the same man.

**Him**   I rush notes for the meeting and do the best I can.

**Her**   I hate him.
And as I accept his apology
I snap a pen in my hand.

**Him**   She just looked at me.
It's not like I was even driving the fucking bus.

**Her**   But before I can really process it
the phone is ringing again
and I don't have time to establish what I think.

**Him**   I don't mean what I said.
I didn't even say it.
I don't mean what I thought.

**Her**   My mind wanders
because it has nothing to cling on to.

**Him**   Just because I think it
it doesn't mean I mean it.

**Her**   I stand in front of the mirror in the toilet.
I wonder how I'm seen by other people.
I am not fat but I trick myself that I am.

**Him**   My dad texts and asks for money
to pay for Mum's Christmas present.
I can't say no.
I tell Frank that I'll go for a pint.

**Her**   I realise I forgot to open the bills in my bag.
Fuck it.

**Him**   The day doesn't come to a neat finish
it just ends because it has to.

**Her**   And I wish my boss a Merry Christmas.

*End of Two.*

**Three**

**He** *appears in a pub.*

**Him**    The pub is busy but Frank doesn't notice.
He doesn't take in his environment
like the rest of us.
There is nothing that touches him
because nothing is real.

We talk about the football.
About the cricket.
Everyone's shit.
They're all playing shit.

Frank's great.
It's all gone wrong for him.

And yet he sits in the office and says nothing.
Just keeps to himself.
But with that he sees everything.

Working with a man so apathetic
is both exciting and dangerous.

I tell him that me and her are stronger than ever.
I tell him that I've only just realised
how important it is to be together
in times like these.
And how close we were
to making the biggest mistake of our lives.

He tells me he thinks he's ill.
There's nothing wrong with him yet
but he knows it's there.
There's nothing physically wrong
with the milk in your fridge
but you know it'll go off.
There's nothing physically wrong
with that loaf of bread in your cupboard
but that'll get mouldy.

Sometimes you can just feel it.
It's already within us, our deaths.

Fucking hell, Frank. I say.
That's a bit heavy.

You start wondering about tomorrow.
You start wondering about how much hope
you can put on it.

I can't be doing with this, he says.
I'm trapped here.
It's a bloody prison.
There's no better word for it.
Prison.
I ask him what he means.
The pub?
The office?
No, he says.
Here.
And he taps the side of his head.
Here.

We realise it's easier on both of us
if nothing is said.
And so we just sit there and finish our drinks.
Merry Christmas, Frank.
Cheers.

*End of Three.*


**Four**

**She** *appears, decorating a Christmas tree with pristine ornaments.*
**She** *strings fairy lights around the branches.*

**He** *appears.*

**Her**   Do you know what I believe in?

**Him**   What do you believe in?

**Her**    I believe in this.
I believe in here.
Me and you.

**She** *continues to decorate the tree.*

**Him**    We have a good Christmas.
We spend it alone.
We spend it together.

**Her**    I tell my mother we're just having a quiet one.
You know how busy he's been
and what with the year we've had
He just wants to . . . I just need to relax.

**Him**    We greet morning gently
with the natural waking of our bodies.
We make it through the day
and the world doesn't collapse.
The telephone doesn't ring
and the television is ignored.
And in this space two humans can exist
and be themselves.

**She** *is on the phone.*

**Her**    It was great.
It was like going away.
Which is weird because we were just at home.
Home.
I've never called this place home before.

**Him**    I buy her a necklace of white gold.

**She** *holds the necklace.*

**Her**    I love it.
Can you help me?

**He** *helps put it on* **Her.**

**Her**    Do you like yours?

**Him**   She bought me a watch
that tells the time on every continent.

I tell her I love it.
Though I am cold to it.
It's just a necklace.
It's just a watch.

**Her**   It stresses me.
We are not cheap people and
we will start the New Year with new debts.

**Him**   But it's Christmas.
Fucking Christmas.
And we're taking time out for ourselves.

**Her**   It was then when we realised
how content we could be
if we could just be left alone.

*End of Four.*


**Five**

*They appear.*

**Him**   At New Year we are required to join our friends
Nick and Chloe for a night out
that has been planned for months.

**Her**   We don't have to if you don't want to.

**Him**   I lie and tell her I am looking forward to it.
Truth is Christmas alone was bliss.
Us against the world.
Outside and tomorrow come too soon.
But you can't stay indoors forever.

**Her**   They take us to the adult crèches
naively called Revolution
Panache and Utopia.

**Him**    She suggests a pill to make it easy on ourselves.
To have a good time.
The chemical wash fooling us
that this is somewhere close to happy.

I am twenty-nine years old.
I am popular.
I am handsome.
I have a loving girlfriend and I am set for life.

**Her**    I am twenty-seven.
I would cross a burning bridge for him.
My mother is proud of me.
I can abide my job and I trust my friends.
I am set for life.

**Him**    She dances like a dreamer.
The number of times we have almost given up
is the number of near fatal mistakes
I have made in my life. Do you want a drink?

**Her**    I see the looks he gets.
Chloe reminds me that he is a keeper.

Though I don't think that I am ugly
I believe myself to be dull and boring and plain.

**Him**    Elbows as sharp as maths digging into the side.
As the barman chooses who to serve
the griping and groaning herd rub across each other.
The powdered sluts and cunts.
I hate this.
This is not me.

**Her**    I don't enjoy going out.
I do it for him.
I believe this is what he wants.
But I watch him.
And just for a moment
for a split second

I see it in his face
that he is not happy here either.

I tell him.
I don't know why
but it feels right to be honest
and to let him know
that I don't think our friends understand us.
And that I'd like to go home.

**Him**    Are you OK? I ask.

**Her**    Yes, I say.

**Him**    I want to go home too.

*End of Five.*


**Six**

*They are sitting on the pavement outside their flat.*

*They are lit by a clock of light which is close to midnight.*

**Him**    And we left.
Dodging the queues and crowds
spilt drinks, broken glass and street fighters.

**Her**    I love you.
You are warmer than you'll ever know.

**Him**    Midnight.

**Her**    A new year.

**Him**    Brought in with mugs of white wine.
Watching other people's fireworks.

**Her**    And we are alone.

**Him**    Together.

**Her**    We find ourselves a space.

**Him**    The idea of being here and nothing else.
Able to take what we want as what we are.

**Her**    I miss myself terribly.
I've got nothing to say to myself any more.

**Him**    And I tell to her that Christmas
meant more to me than . . .

**Her**    And I've never been happier than . . .

**Him**    And I can't stop thinking about when . . .

**Her**    And why should we be ashamed
of wanting to spend time alone.
I fucking love you.

**Him**    All we can do in this life
is make a little room for ourselves.
That's our own little space.
We can make clocks that never tick.

**Her**    If the moment calls we can tell it to wait.

**Him**    And we sat there at midnight
and watched the New Year roll in.
New stars and ideas.
We sat with each other
both agreeing that there's nothing purer
than fresh rain
after being stuck out in the rotten air.

*The clock strikes midnight. End of Six.*

**Seven**

*They appear.*

**Her**    Wake up.

**Him**    Wake up.

**Her**    I make a cup of tea.
And as the kettle boils I stare out of the window
and think of nothing.
I literally think of nothing.

**Him**    I'm being battered by the pattern.

**Her**    At work each phone call is abuse.
Each email is a threat.
Or at least that's how it feels.
But if it feels like that then surely that's how it is.

**Him**    I watch hardcore pornography
rather than edit a report.

**Her**    I go to the bathroom and check my hair.
I look at myself in the same way
other people look at the television.
Not watching.
Letting it rinse over my eyes.

**Him**    I accidently download another virus.
It freezes my computer.

**Her**    I make cups of tea.
And pour them in the sink.

**Him**    Work dulls me to a nub
so that I only walk to the door
where in the past I used to run.

**Her**    My mum worries that we're struggling for money.
His dad is still out of work
and the rain outside never stops.
She asks me how I feel and I'm sure
she's anticipating me to be sad or depressed
but I'm happy because I've got him.

**Him**    Frank hasn't made it into work.
I ask around if anyone knows why
but by the looks on their faces
they barely know who the fuck I'm on about.

**Her**    I get another call for the phone bill.
I accidentally answer it and hang up straight away.
Fuck.
Steven from accounts comes over
and tells me he likes my hair today.

**Him**   I think about the old man.
I didn't realise how much I need him here.

**Her**   I overhear him later on
telling Adam from accounts
how he'd like to wreck me
and hang out the back of me
and smash my back door in.

**Him**   Perhaps I see him as an older me.
Or what I could see myself being if I'm not careful.

**Her**   The violence in their language confuses me.
It takes me a moment to realise they mean sex.
And suddenly I'm aware of every cock in the room.

**Him**   I look through his desk and drawers
to see what kind of shit I'll horde
when I'm his age and sat here.

**Her**   I'm a bit embarrassed.
A bit coy.
A bit fucking angry.

**Him**   And I see that he has nothing in his desk.
His cupboards are empty.
I can't believe it and I admire the old bastard.

**Her**   I think about my legs.
I think about my eyes.

**Him**   He sits here all day and he doesn't let it touch him.
His empty desk nothing but a vessel
of the all the fucks he gives.

**Her**   I think about myself in parts.

**Him**   I look around the office
and Frank may be old and sad
but at least he doesn't believe in this.

**Her**   Somebody in the office tells a joke.
I check myself as I smile.

**Him**   For some people normal isn't enough.
For some people this isn't enough.

**Her**   And I ask myself
What are you smiling at?
What are you actually smiling at?

**Him**   I'm not happy and I'm not sad.
I'm just fucking there.

**Her**   I'm asked to take minutes for a meeting upstairs
and they're taking the piss.

**Him**   I'm not becoming the man I thought I'd become.

**Her**   If they had balls
then they'd tell me to take the minutes.
Who the fuck are you asking me to take minutes?

**Him**   I get a text from my dad telling me the money
I tried to transfer didn't go through.
I check my account online and I haven't enough.

**Her**   Fuck you asking.
Tell me.
Tell me to take your fucking minutes.

**Him**   He's bled me dry.

**Her**   I sit there in silence.

**Him**   I see the cars outside my window.
Wishing for a crash.
Something to happen.
Something like breaking glass.

**Her**   I stop listening.

**Him**   Just for a moment.

**Her**   It is silent.

**Him**   Go home.

**Her**   Go home.

**Him**    Today I have realised . . .

**Her**    Today I have realised . . .

**Him**    It is possible for Frank to exist yet not be in work.

**Her**    I've never sat comfortably at my desk.

**Him**    It is possible to just say no.

**Her**    That maybe I should start saying no.

*End of Seven.*


**Eight**

*They are sitting at a table. They have been eating.*

**Him**    There are children getting caught in the war.
    Little starving bombed children
    that will die after barely being born.
    That child will die pure.
    And his little legs and his little arms
    his little face and his little arse
    are being blown to bits by adults.

**Her**    Did you have a good day?

**Him**    Yeah.
    You?

**Her**    Yeah.

**She** *goes to clear the table.* **He** *stops* **Her**, *as to say not to bother.*
*Pause.*

**He** *goes to hold* **Her** *hand but as* **He** *reaches over the table* **He**
*knocks a glass.*

*The moment* **He** *struggled to create is broken.* **He** *is resigned to let*
**Her** *stack the plates, the cutlery and the glasses.*

**She** *takes them to the sink. Moment.*

*The television, in another space, switches on. It is white noise and 'snow'.*

**Him**   I tried to transfer money to my dad
and there wasn't enough.

**Her**   How much more does he want?

**Him**   A bit.

**Her**   A bit . . .

**Him**   Just a bit more.
They have to live.

**Her**   We can hardly manage.

**Him**   We should be fine.

**Her**   Well, we're not.

**Him**   Both of us are working.

**Her**   Council tax has gone up.
Rent has gone up.
Fucking draining money to your parents.

**Him**   I can't help that.

**Her**   Yeah, well we can't help
having the heating on either.

I start to open the letters at work.
One after another asking for more
and asking more often.
No let up.
No consideration.
No more warnings.

Your phone is going to default.
I can't do it because it's in your name.

**Him**   Right.

**Her**   You need to tell them we can't pay it yet.

**Him**  Yet . . .

**Her**  Well, what the fuck do you want me to do?
Take your watch back?

**Him**  Yeah.

**Her**  Fuck you.

**Him**  I don't understand how we can't afford . . . We're on
good wages.

**Her**  Not good enough.

*End of Eight.*


### Nine

*They are faced with a mountain of bills.*

*They start burying mounds and mounds of letters in any crevice they
can find in their flat.*

*The place is fit to bursting. End of Nine.*


### Ten

**He** *appears.*

**Him**  First I thought she'd fucked up.
I mean I know I leave it to her
but we work and that should be enough.
If you work then you should be able to afford to . . .
I mean yeah, I've had to lend my parents a few quid
but you can afford that.
You should be able to afford that.

My dad calls with good news.
He's got a job.
I ask him what doing.
It's picking litter in a park.

You can just imagine him there.
These little shits.
Little bastards dropping rubbish everywhere.
And there's my dad behind
picking up after them.
If they shat on the pavement
would he have to pick that up too?

The war today spread
to the neighbouring provinces.
The civil outbreak has caused
the international community
to condemn the people for fighting for their lives.
They've never seen fire in Geneva.

I read an article online
about a Spaniard who shot himself and his family.

They say he was deranged.
Say he had issues.

Though the reasons he shot himself they report
were mounting debts, the loss of his job
troubles with alcohol dependency
and pressures at home.

Now that to me doesn't sound like derangement.
To me that sounds like
the whole fucking world falling in on him.

**She** *appears.*

**Her**   And you think shooting yourself and your family
is the right way of dealing with those problems?

**Him**   I didn't say that.
But let's not make it something it wasn't.
He was failed.
Then he failed his family.
In that order.

Frank has still not turned up for work.
I have taken to drinking out of his mug.

**Her**    The walls in the flat.
　　They weren't painted that long ago.
　　The landlord talks about painting them again.
　　But with every layer of paint he coats the walls
　　the smaller it makes the room.
　　Each layer is another crust.
　　I can feel the room closing in.
　　At what point do you say something?
　　At what point do you refuse?

　　I dream about Steven from accounts
　　and Adam from accounts
　　taking it in turns to smash me
　　while my boyfriend watches.

　　Can you ring O2?
　　Can you do something about these fucking bills?

**Him**    Yeah.

**Her**    I can't deal with it on my own.

**Him**    I know.
　　You don't have to.

*End of Ten.*


**Eleven**

**He** *appears.*

**Him**    I wake up.

**She** *appears.*

**Her**    He rings me at work.

**Him**    I phone her.

**Her**    How are you feeling?

**Him**    I lie.

**Her**    Well, I hope you feel better, darling.
    Are you going to try and make it into work?

**Him**    I lie again.

**Her**    OK, see you later.

**She** *disappears.*

**Him**    I sit in my dressing gown
    eating cold soup out of a can.
    I wasn't ill though this makes me feel sick.

The only actual work I do all day
is writing on internet forums.
I say controversial things to provoke a response.
I incite anger using racism, sexism, homophobia.
I blame the Jews for the markets crashing.
I blame the Muslims for pretty much
everything else.
I masterfully litter my tirades
with spelling mistakes
and factual inaccuracies, circular logic
and ignorance.
Though I do not believe anything that I am saying
I find this much more exciting and rewarding
than work ever was.
There's a cooking programme on the television
and some of the men there are crying.

I phone Frank.
A young man answers.
It's his son or something.
Frank's been taken ill.
He's in hospital.
I say thank you and hang up the phone.

I didn't really listen.
I said thank you
before I hung up the phone.

*End of Eleven.*

**Twelve**

**She** *is in the mirror.*

**She** *is putting make-up on.*

**She** *finishes and looks at herself. She is pretty.*

**She** *wipes her hand across her face, taking the lipstick with it.*

**She** *wipes her eyes, her cheeks.*

**She** *scruffs her hair.* **She** *looks ridiculous.* **He** *appears on the phone.*

**Him**    I ring the company like she asked me to.
I'm phoning with regards to . . .
They know why I'm phoning.
I have a problem with the . . .
They know what my problem is.

Can you help?
They can't help.
The barking echoes of terms and conditions.
The policies and the packages.
The contracts and the clauses.
They cannot help.

Frank is dying
I tell them.
And I said thank you.
'Who's Frank?' they ask me.

**Her**    At work I am stared at.
I am asked if I am OK.
Yes, I say.
Yes I am thank you, how are you?

**Him**    I'm Frank, I say.
I know I'm Frank because I hate it too.
Because I can't pretend to give a shit.
And if I'm not Frank yet then I will be.

'Would you like us to call you back
at a more convenient time?'

**Her**   I hear Adam from accounts
talking to Steven from accounts.
Asking what have I done with myself.
At no point do they mention
the prospect of fucking me.

**Him**   I tell him that we're not paying.
He tells me I am contracted.
I tell him that I'll cancel my direct debit.
He tells me they'll cut me off.
I tell him I'll sell the phone.
He tells me I can't do that.
I tell him that I think he overestimates his position.

**Her**   I'm asked to see the boss.
He asks me what's wrong.
I tell him nothing.
He says that he considers me a hard worker.
I ask him if he's called me in
because I don't look fuckable.
He smiles.
A smile that I believe means
that he could still fuck me if he wanted to.

**Him**   He tells me I have to continue paying the bill.
He tells me they are providing a service.
That this is how the world works.

I ask him if he's ever allowed himself to be alive.
I ask him if he's ever said no
to anything he's ever been told.

Imagine saying no as a concept.
Yes is passive.
No is refusal.
Yes is acceptance.
No is an action.
Yes is dire.
No is a new idea.

**Her**    I take the afternoon off on recommendation.
I'm asked to consider how I dress for work
and the importance of good presentation.
I will not present myself to you, I think.
But I smile.
And I shake his hand.

**Him**    I tell him to fuck off.
Not the company.
Him.
Personally.
You.
Fuck off.

**Her**    I just want to be home.

*End of Twelve.*

**Thirteen**

**He** *appears at Frank's bedside.*

**Him**    Frank sat amongst tubes.
And he's happy to see me.

We talk about the football.
About the cricket.
Everyone's shit.
They're all playing shit.

He tells me he has days.
But it has taken years to get to this point.
He asks me if I'm happy.
I tell him that I haven't thought about it.
He tells me I don't ask enough questions.
I tell him I do, just not out loud.

He tells me that something comes over you
when you're near the end.
Memories seem to have much more relevance
because they're all you have.

And you put everything in its own little box . . .
And then you realise that some boxes
those labelled disappointment and regret
are full to the brim
And those labelled love and happiness
are almost empty in comparison.

He's angry.
He's fucking furious.
He's wasted his entire life.
And what he's dying of isn't cancer
but other people.

Start asking questions.

*End of Thirteen.*


### Fourteen

*They appear.*

**Him**    Are you happy?

**Her**    What?

**Him**    You need to answer me the question
Are you happy
Without any thought or pause
Are you happy
And if you have to think
Then it means you're not
Answer the question
Are you happy
Quick
Are you happy
Go.

**Her**    I . . .

**Him**    No.
Neither am I.

**Her**    What's brought this on?

**Him**    Something Frank said.

**Her**    How is he?

**Him**    Dead.

*End of Act Two.*

## Act Three

### One

**He** *appears.*

**Him**    There are moments in the day
   where I believe that I am all.

   Where the light breathes from me.
   And the cold cools only me.

   There are moments in the day
   where time ticks just for me
   and I watch the past
   and present dance, dissolve in duet.

   Where strangers weep and I see them
   and I believe their tears are shed for me.

   I close my eyes
   and I can still make out the world
   as if my eyes were open.

   I sit in spaces left alone.

   Here are your playgrounds
   your parks and your peace.
   Watch the rain pour on to them
   and settle on the surface
   unable to soak into the ground.

   There are moments in the day
   where I believe that I am all.

   They are getting fewer.
   And I know I cannot last.

*End of One.*

**Two**

**He** *is in a space.*

**She** *appears.*

**He** *takes a sandwich out of its box, takes it apart and only eats the meat within it.*

**She** *takes a sandwich out of its box, takes it apart but can find nothing within it that she wants to eat.*

*End of Two.*


**Three**

*They appear.*

**Her**    Wake up.

**Him**    Wake up.

**Her**    Kettle on.

**Him**    Turn over.

**Her**    Forgot my fucking slippers.

**Him**    Back asleep.

**Her**    Get up.

**Him**    No.

**Her**    Even with the TV off
the brash bang and flash of war dominate the flat.
I do nothing as the clock passes nine.

**Him**    Good morning.

**Her**    We're running late.

**Him**    My phone alarm.
It didn't go off.

**Her**    Didn't set it.

**Him**    Yeah.

**Her**    So . . .
   What shall we do?

**Him**    We fuck.

**Her**    His mobile rings.

**Him**    Mid-coitus.

**Her**    Answer it.

**Him**    No.

**Her**    Could be important.

**Him**    It isn't.

**Her**    Could be.

**Him**    I answer it.

**Her**    It's O2.

**Him**    I hang up.

**Her**    What was it?

**Him**    Don't care.

**Her**    And then he . . .

**Him**    Then I just . . .

**Her**    He threw his phone.

**Him**    Smash.

**Her**    Against the wall.

**Him**    Fuck it all.

**Her**    Broke.

**Him**    Yeah.

**Her**    But . . . .

**Him**    Don't need it.

**Her**   Yeah.

**Him**   We fuck again.

**Her**   Get to work three hours late.
I pretend to have a cold.

**Him**   I wander in without showering
and not wearing a tie.
I get looks at reception.
I know they will be talking about me.

**Her**   I smell of sex.
His cum pooled and drying in my knickers.
I am not owned by the company.

**Him**   Stinks of bleach.
The cleaners have been in.
My desk could do with a deeper scrub.
Erode it like a coast.

**Her**   I do one thing an hour.
No one notices if I don't kill myself working.
A revelation.

**Him**   I am not asked about my lateness
or my appearance.

**Her**   I overhear Adam from accounts
and Steven from accounts talking.
The new girl Hannah is being rated.

**Him**   There is an argument
about Frank's job description.
They are putting an ad in an agency.
Turns out no one really knew what he did.

**Her**   Thanks to her chest and arse she is welcome.

**Him**   I haven't brushed my teeth.

**Her**   She's a cute girl.
I unplug my phone.

**Him**    I read opinion pieces on the war.
   Nobody understands it.
   They're all talking politics.
   But out there.
   On the front line.
   It's reality.
   This isn't it.
   This isn't real.
   We won't die here.
   Nothing's on the line.
   It's a fucking office.

**Her**    I feel sorry for the girl but I am glad she is here
   to soak up the attention.

**Him**    I start browsing hardcore porn sites
   while I look for news on the war.
   A common theme.
   Life.

**Her**    She might enjoy it now.
   But she's new.
   She'll get over it.
   She'll resent it.

**Him**    I confuse myself and feel sick.

**Her**    And she'll resent herself for enjoying it.

**Him**    I smoke a cigarette in the car park.
   Fuck it.
   The day's too long for me.

**Her**    The slut.

**Him**    I spend the afternoon asleep in the toilet.
   I wake to pick her up and we go home.

**Her**    Gets what she deserves.

**Him**    And like breathing in without chest bones
   we are relieved.

**Her**    I smile as I leave the office.
You all get what you deserve.

**Him**    Today I have realised . . .

**Her**    Today I have realised . . .

**Him**    I make no effort with my life.

**Her**    I could disappear.
And no one would notice.

**Him**    I hate almost everyone.
Other than her.

**Her**    I've worried about my job for so long.

**Him**    And maybe myself.

**Her**    But I've been shown it doesn't matter.

**Him**    Maybe.

**Her**    And neither do I.

*End of Three.*


**Four**

*They appear.*

**Him**    Wake up.

**Her**    Wake up.

*Long silence. End of Four.*


**Five**

*They appear.*

**Her**    Wake up.

**Him**    We fuck for hours
and get into work
for the afternoon.

**Her**   I get to the office eventually but no one cares.
I sit there and don't know what point I'm making.

**Him**   Fuck it.

**Her**   While he is still inside me
I feel like two people.

**Him**   I break my desk cupboard.

**Her**   I have no respect.

**Him**   On my lunch I go to the market.

**Her**   I spit a little bit in the kettle.

**Him**   I take a box of rancid fruit
that has been left out in the bins.

**Her**   I am asked to photocopy a contract.

**Him**   I hide fetid bananas
soft apples
and bad oranges
in the office.

**Her**   I copy the front page and the back page.

**Him**   Within hours the place stinks like a drain.

**Her**   And fill it with blank pages.

**Him**   The flies will be here tomorrow.

**Her**   I hand the contract back to my boss.
I hold eye contact with him
so that when he looks back
he will know it was intentional.

**Him**   I will deny any knowledge
of where the smell comes from.

**Her**   But he doesn't notice.

**Him**   I suggest wryly
that's it Frank haunting us.
But it's me.
It's me haunting them.

**Her**    And that is testament to my worth.

**Him**    I ask the office
what the fuck they're doing.
Frank practically died here.
I'm not going to let it get me.
This is not my life's work.

**Her**    I accost Adam from accounts.
I tell him that I'd fuck him.
And I'd fucking ruin him.
The fucking cunt.

*They walk off. End of Five.*

**Six**

**He** *appears.*

**Him**    I ring my dad.
He tells me he's on his break.
I ask him how much shit he's picked up today.
How many used condoms.
Tampons.
Knives.
Needles.
Nappies.
Dog shit.
Horse shit.
Rat shit.
Dead rats.
Dead dogs.
Dead horses.
He tells me I'm putting him off his biscuits.
I tell him he's putting me off the future.
I ask him what the fuck he's doing.
And he hangs up the phone.

I dial his number again
and this time he doesn't even say hello

he just picks up
and I tell him
he can keep the fucking money he owes me
because I don't fucking need it.
I shit money.
I ooze money.
This time I hang up
and I go to the kitchen to smash a cup.

**He** *walks out.*

**Her**    I dream again of Steven from accounts
having sex with me.
But this time
I turn and pull his cock
and keep pulling
until it just rips off in my hand.
And I don't know what to do with it
I'm just there with this little bloody cock
in my hand
and I'm not even dreaming it
I'm awake and stood in the middle of the office
and muttering to myself
and maybe . . .

**He** *rushes on, grabs* **Her** *and they run off stage laughing and wrestling. End of Six.*


**Seven**

*They are at a table.*

**Him**    How was your day?

**Her**    Good.

**Him**    What made it good?

*The telephone rings. They try to ignore it.*

*It gets louder and louder.*

**He** *picks it up.*

**Him**   O2 call the landline
they tell me that for days
they have been trying to get hold of me.
The bill is still outstanding.
And I tell them I'll show you something
fucking outstanding
but they don't get that I mean my cock
and they don't get that it's a joke.

I tell them that the phone is broken.
How is it broken?
I broke it.
Your warranty won't cover that.

Are you happy with your life?
I ask him.
Stunned.
Emotion down the telephone.
A soft touch right to the centre of his heart.

**He** *takes a pair of scissors.*

**He** *playfully snips the air with them.* **She** *is nervous.*

I tell him that everything I care about in my life
is transient and temporary.
The love I have for her
cannot be measured or sold.
It cannot be touched or sullied
and it exists only if I say it does.

I love her
and what she represents.

**He** *cuts the line.* **She** *is relieved. They kiss.*

*End of Seven.*

**Eight**

*They appear.*

**Him**    Liberated by the cut phone
I suggest we flood the kitchen.

**Her**    I tell him to calm down
and maybe we should look in the catalogue
for a new telephone.

**Him**    Who do you need to ring?

**Her**    What?

**Him**    Who do you need to phone?

**Her**    No one.
I don't know.
At some point.

**Him**    Well, we'll worry about it then.
Didn't it feel good?
Didn't it feel a relief?

**Her**    I suppose it was.
And it was.
I felt three stone lighter the moment he cut it.

**Him**    I broke a cup at work
and it felt just like this
and I thought
at the time
it was the cup
but it was me and how I felt
and I feel the same now
do you get what I mean.
It isn't about the stuff
It's about . . .

**He** *takes a plate and drops it on the floor. It smashes everywhere.*

**Her**    Careful!
What are you doing?

**He** *smashes another one.*

**Him**    Don't you see what I mean?
  It's just stuff.

**He** *passes her a plate.* **She** *thinks about it.* **She** *drops it on the floor.*

**She** *stifles an embarrassed laugh. End of Eight.*


### Nine

*They appear.*

*They lay out tools from carrier bags.*

*They destroy and dismantle everything in their flat.*

**She** *sits on the floor and cuts up photographs while* **He** *breaks the table into pieces.*

**He** *rips down the centre of the sofa.*

**She** *destroys her necklace with a hammer.* **He** *watches.*

**He** *takes his watch off and stamps on it.* **She** *watches.*

*The television is still blaring the war.* **He** *takes the hammer to it. End of Nine.*


### Ten

*Lights rise on the mess. End of Ten.*


### Eleven

*They are in a bath. They are fully clothed.*

**She** *reads from a book.* **She** *rips pages out of it.*

**Him**    Dream in shatters.
  Dream in frost.

  Dream of people watching.

**He** *touches* **Her** *face,* **Her** *cheek.*

You are enormously significant
to my existence.

I could count on my hand
all the things I live for.
There's nothing else after the forefinger.
You are the thumb.

**She** *bites* **His** *thumb. They kiss.*

*End of Eleven.*


### Twelve

*Lights up on them fucking.*

*They ignore the scene that they're meant to be doing. She comes.*

*End of Twelve.*


### Thirteen

*They appear.*

**Him**    Wake up.

**Her**    Wake up.

**He** *corpses and* **She** *starts laughing too. The scene breaks down.*

*End of Thirteen.*


### Fourteen

*They appear.*

**Him**    Wake up.

**Her**    Wake up.

**Him**    How did you sleep?

**Her**    Deep.

**Him**    I watch her get up.
  Her shorts.

**Her**    There are no mugs for tea.
  There is no toaster for toast.
  I don't know what to do about breakfast.

**Him**    We go back to sleep.

*End of Fourteen.*


**Fifteen**

*They appear.*

**Her**    Wake up.

**Him**    Yeah.

**Her**    I regret the decision to smash all the lightbulbs
  out of their sockets.

**Him**    The further into the dark she goes
  the harder it is to hear her.

**Her**    The curtains are drawn and the glow of the street
  lights the room in a deep blue and orange.

**Him**    I call for her.

**Her**    I notice something.
  His watch no longer ticks.
  Hands suspended.
  Stuck at quarter past four.

**Him**    I'm not totally convinced I'm awake.

**Her**    The time we decided.

**Him**    I don't know.

**Her**    The time we snapped.

**Him**    What are you doing?

**Her**   Nothing.

**Him**   I'm hungry.
I'm going to find something.

**Her**   Watch your feet.

**Him**   Nothing stands out as edible.

**Her**   And so I sit here in the dark
and maybe that's what he means by escape.

**Him**   Through the blind I see the moon.
I don't see its point.

**Her**   The space daunts me.

**Him**   I don't know what else we need.

**Her**   And so I do nothing.

**Him**   There is nothing else we need.

**Her**   It is easy to get lost here.

**Him**   I don't believe in outside any more.

**Her**   The hallways are daunting.
The shadows deepen.

**Him**   In and out is not sustainable.

**Her**   I'm losing time.

**Him**   Honing my life down into the flat.
Into the room
into the chair
into the head and the eye.

**Her**   I understand what freedom means.

**Him**   I am focused.

**Her**   And what it costs.

*End of Fifteen.*

**Sixteen**

**She** *appears.*

**He** *appears.* **He** *is pissing.*

**She** *tries to find a space where* **She** *can piss.* **She** *can't.*

**He** *finishes and walks away.*

**She** *goes to where* **He** *pissed and pisses there herself. End of Sixteen.*


**Seventeen**

**He** *appears.*

**Him**   I dream of a child hurt
and I can't remember
if I saw him on the news
or I just made him up.
I swear he's hiding in the living room.

I haven't followed the war for a day or so.
Lag of understanding.
But I feel I know which way
the violence drifts.

**She** *appears.*

**Her**   The flat starts to smell.
A fetid and warm-smelling bin.
Crawling through the hall.

**Him**   The longest day of the year
and you can't even
stand the sight yourself
on the shortest days.

**Her**   The clock is irrelevant.

**Him**   Sick of fancy fucking living.
The bourgeois mornings and the predatory afternoons.
The hospitals are open every day.
The morgues close on weekends.
The fuck does that mean.

**Her**   We will get hungry
    or we'll get thirsty
    and get tired of drinking from the tap.
    But we don't think of that now.
    We don't think of that.
    We don't think.
    We don't.
    Don't.

**Him**   Grenades for your dinner.
    Fuck your diet.
    Kill yourself.

*End of Seventeen.*


**Eighteen**

**She** *appears, sifting through a broken cabinet.*

**He** *appears.*

**Him**   What you doing?

**Her**   Headache.

**Him**   Oh.

**Her**   Need something.

**Him**   Yeah?

**Her**   Yeah.
    Don't we have –

**Him**   Just sleep.

**Her**   Can't sleep.
    That's why I'm fucking looking.

**Him**   Alright.

**She** *gives up.*

**Her**   I'll have to go to the shop.

**Him**   What?

**Her**    I can't fucking . . .
I need to go.

**Him**    No. Look. Be fine.

**Her**    In pain.

**Him**    Nothing out there.

**Her**    Please.

**Him**    Nothing for us.
Not any more.
They'll spit in your tea.
Collins cunts.

**Her**    All the food in the tins is rotten.
Muggy rooms.
There's a heat in the bathroom,
I can't find where it's coming from.

**Him**    I want to blacken the walls and grow trees.
I can't grow them alone.
Will you help?

**Her**    I couldn't make any sense out of what he was saying.

**Him**    He was holding him like this.
And he was . . . you know.
But he was holding him like this
and they were in front of trees.

**Her**    And I realised he meant the war.
He wanted to recreate the war at home.

*End of Eighteen.*


**Nineteen**

*They appear.*

**Her**    Wake up.

Cannot sleep.
Cannot dream.

Sit and stare into light purple
early morning.

Bore a hole in the wall.

I saved my mobile when we started breaking stuff.

Call my mum
because I had to talk to someone.
The muffled plastic-smelling tone
of the telephone
is better than nothing.

She told me she was worried.
I told her I was fine.
She told me her and the cat miss me.
And I told her I miss them too.
She asked when I would be home.
She told me she had made my bed.
She had made me cheese on toast
and a cup of tea.
She asked again when I would be home.
At least I've spoken out loud today.

He tells me he cannot think.
He sits and vegetates.
I have noticed his eyes
go from a blue to a grey.

I feel him drifting further.
A broken buoy at sea.

**Him**    Wake up.

**Her**    Open a can of beans.

**Him**    Feel her gone.

**Her**    Sit and stare at the smashed television.

**Him**    Walk through to living room.

**Her**    The silence soothing.

**Him**    Are you alright?

**Her**    Yeah.

**Him**    You're up.

**Her**    I check my face in the cracked mirror.

**Him**    Come back to bed.

**Her**    I can't sleep.

**Him**    I can't wake up.

**Her**    Go back to bed.

**Him**    Are you alright?

**Her**    I watch the sun rise.

**Him**    Asleep in seconds.

**Her**    I feel alone in this house.

**Him**    All my energy is facing upward.

**Her**    I didn't realise things would be so fucking intense.

**Him**    I hear her crying.

**Her**    And I wonder if we're going in the same direction or if I'm just following him.

*End of Nineteen.*


**Twenty**

**He** *is lit by holding a lamp that's still working.* **He** *drops it on the floor and the light goes out. End of Twenty.*


**Twenty-One**

*They appear.*

**Her**    What are you eating?

**Him**    I made us food.

**Her**    What is it?

**Him**    I made it in the kitchen.

**Her**    I don't know.

**Him**    I made it for us.

**Her**    But I don't know if I can eat it.
I don't know if I should.

**Him**    We've eaten worse.

**Her**    It smells.
It's not right.

**Him**    All we can do in this life
is make a little room for ourselves.
That's our own little space.
We can make clocks that never tick.
Take what we want as . . .

**Her**    And is this what we want?

**Him**    Yes.

**Her**    I thought this was about us.

**Him**    Everything's about us.

**Her**    I don't think we can cope with that.

*End of Twenty-One.*


### Twenty-Two

**She** *is picking through mountains of old sandwich boxes, looking for food within them.*

**She** *is struggling and gets frustrated.*

**He** *appears with a can of beans but they can't open it.*

**He** *starts to eat bits of the cardboard from the sandwich boxes.*

**She** *is reluctant to join him. End of Twenty-Two.*

**Twenty-Three**

*They appear.*

**Him**    Do you think that's what they say?
Do you think that's what they're saying
to each other
right fucking now?

**Her**    Who?

**Him**    Them.

**Her**    You don't turn to me any more.

**Him**    No.

**Her**    You think what you have is growing.

**Him**    It is.

**Her**    I've stopped dreaming.

**Him**    I'm not enough for you.

**Her**    I rang my mum.

**Him**    Right.

**Her**    I think I need to go away.

**Him**    I want us to have a baby.
In here.
Will you let me fuck you?

**Her**    No.

**Him**    I think you're being unreasonable.

*End of Twenty-Three.*


**Twenty-Four**

**She** *is putting lipstick on.*

*After* **She** *has finished* **She** *takes a bite from the stick and eats it.*
*End of Twenty-Four.*

**Twenty-Five**

**She** *is sitting on the floor, a blanket wrapped around her.*

**He** *is standing.*

**Him**   We're at war.
  Me and you.

**Her**   Fuck.

**Him**   I suggest we blind ourselves.
  In a moment of inspired idiocy
  I ask her to gouge out my eyes
  with a knife.
  There's only so far you can go for someone.
  Tears pouring down her face.

**Her**   I'm scared of you.

**She** *gets up.*

**She** *goes to* **Him**.

  I'm sorry.
  I didn't mean it.
  But I did.
  I don't know why I'm here.
  He is four miles away from me.

  I think it's just relief.
  I was at my lowest.
  Maybe I still am.
  But that's not to say
  I'm going to stay this low for ever.

  We're losing each other.
  How can this happen?
  What do we do?
  What the fuck do we do?

**Him**   Nothing.

**Her**   My mum has asked me to go home.

**Him**    I know.

**Her**    How do you know?

**Him**    I can see in your eyes.
You've already gone.

*End of Twenty-Five.*


**Twenty-Six**

**She** *has bags.*

**Her**    You could come with me.
Do you want to come with me?

**Him**    I spent the night looking through old cut up photos
of you as a child
and they are happy.
That's all you are really.

**Her**    If you're lost then you need to say
because if I come to find you
I might not know the way back.

**Him**    That's OK.

**Her**    What do you think you are achieving?

**Him**    Nothing.

**Her**    I do not tell him that as soon as I leave
I will phone the police
and an ambulance.

**Him**    We both know where I'm going doesn't exist.
But let's talk as if it does.

**Her**    I love you.

**She** *disappears.*

**Him**    You're amazing
even when you're not here.

**He** *notices* **Her** *gone.*

> There are moments in the day
> where I believe that I am all.

> There is a soft edge to the world
> and there is an understanding between who I am
> and what is expected of me.

*His light fades. The bath is lit.*

**He** *takes his shirt off.*

> There are moments in the day
> where I believe that I am all.

> There are moments in the day
> where I am nothing.

**He** *throws it in the bath.*

**He** *lights a match.*

*The block of light fades, leaving the scene lit only by the match in his hand.*

**He** *throws the match into the bath.*

*The shirt burns.*

# The Brink

*For Al Smith*

## Characters

**Nick**, *twenty-eight – a secondary school teacher*
**Chloe**, *twenty-eight – a project manager*
**Jo**, *thirty-four – a secondary school teacher*
**Mr Boyd**, *forty-three – head teacher at the school*
**Martin**, *thirty-six – Chloe's boss*
**Jessica**, *fifteen – a student*
**One, Two, Three**, *fifteen – students*

*Doubling can occur where necessary, played ideally with a company or four as follows –*

**Nick**
**Chloe/Jessica/student two**
**Jo/student three**
**Mr Boyd/Martin/student one**

*Setting and sound*
Transient, non-naturalistic. Uniform and efficient like a textbook.

*Note on the text*
. . . denotes speech trailing off

/ denotes interruption

## Part One

### One

*The present. Night time.*

**Nick** *is alone on the school field.*

**Nick**   So it starts like any other day. I get up and I shower
and just like any other day I quit my job. Luckily for me I've
never had the courage of my convictions, so by the time I
brush my teeth I've already talked myself down from the
ledge. If I quit teaching I have no idea where I'd end up –
dead, or you know, worse. I never remember the journey to
work, and it's weird because after the shower I'm just there
bang outside the school. And there's fire everywhere. Half
the building's torn to shit. There's nothing left of the Maths
block. It's just fire and cinder and I'm stood there, stood
there watching this yawning hell and I say *what's happened*
and someone says *a bomb's gone off*. And I say *where's a bomb
come from* and they say *the Brink*. But I don't know what that
means. See I've never even heard of the Brink. And so I just
say again, *where the fuck's a bomb come from?*

### Two

*Earlier.*

*It's dark.* **Chloe** *turns the light on. The kitchen.*

**Nick** *is sat eating cereal.*

**Chloe**   'kin hell.

**Nick**   Sorry.

**Chloe**   Sat in the dark. Scared me to shit.

**Nick**   Yeah, sorry.

**Chloe**   What are you doing?

**Nick**  Having breakfast.

**Chloe**  It's half five. Why've you got the light off?

**Nick**  Couldn't sleep. You going for your run?

**Chloe**  Yeah.

*She sits.*

Maybe.

*Beat.*

No.

**Nick**  No?

**Chloe**  I don't think I can do it anymore.

**Nick**  Only started yesterday.

**Chloe**  I just don't think it's me. Day two and I'm already in tears putting my trainers on. Who runs on purpose, for fuck sake? It's perverse.

**Nick**  If you don't enjoy it then don't do it.

**Chloe**  It's not that simple though, is it, Nick? Can't mess around anymore. We're in our late twenties and late twenties might as well be early thirties and early thirties might as well be forties and forties might as well be fifty. We're nearly fucking *fifty*, Nick. We've got to look after ourselves.

**Nick**  Christ. Right. What are you going to do then?

**Chloe**  You can sweat yourself fit. Read about it the other day. I might do that. Don't have to get up early to sweat, do you? Do you want a cup of tea?

**Nick**  Yeah go on.

*She goes to make tea.*

**Chloe**  Was I snoring?

**Nick**  What?

**Chloe**    Are you up because I was snoring?

**Nick**    No, you weren't snoring, no.

*Beat.*

Do you understand your dreams? Like, what they're about.

**Chloe**    Why? What do I say?

**Nick**    Nothing.

**Chloe**    Pretty unfair if you're criticising me for something I say in my sleep.

**Nick**    No, you don't say anything. I'm just asking whether or not you understand what your dreams mean.

**Chloe**    Oh. Well, no. But who does?

**Nick**    So they're just nonsense?

**Chloe**    You can't worry about stupid sex dreams, Nick.

**Nick**    Sex dreams? Where did you get sex dreams from?

**Chloe**    That's what you mean, isn't it? About who you have sex with in your dreams?

**Nick**    No.

**Chloe**    Oh.

**Nick**    You dream about us having sex?

**Chloe**    Well . . .

**Nick**    Who are you having sex with in your dreams, Chloe? Fucking hell.

**Chloe**    I don't know.

**Nick**    How can you not know?

**Chloe**    I don't know. I can't see their faces.

**Nick**    Why can't you see their face? Because it's from behind?

**Chloe**   What?

**Nick**   Do you mean you can't see their face because they're having sex with you from behind?

**Chloe**   Nick, I don't /

**Nick**   / Did you say *face* or *faces*?

**Chloe**   Why does it matter?

**Nick**   I'm just interested. How often do you . . . you know.

**Chloe**   How often do I what? How often do I come?

**Nick**   No. How often do you dream, holy shit, you can come more than once?

**Chloe**   Why are you even asking me? What's this about?

**Nick**   I don't know, I just . . . I just had this dream about the school. About something really bad happening at the school.

**Chloe**   A sex dream at the school?

**Nick**   No. Not a . . . But it was horrible, Chloe. Really dark.

**Chloe**   Christ. You're properly freaked out.

**Nick**   A bit. I mean, it wouldn't mean anything though would it?

**Chloe**   I suppose if it's a one-off . . .

**Nick**   I've had it a few times.

**Chloe**   Right.

**Nick**   It's quite a violent dream. There's a lot of blood. But it can't mean anything. Can it?

**Chloe**   What are you actually doing in the dream?

**Nick**   No, I'm not doing anything. It's not me.

**Chloe**   Oh good.

**Nick**   I'm not like . . .

**Chloe**   No, that's a relief.

**Nick**   Jesus.

**Chloe**   I know. That's what I thought.

**Nick**   But the sight of it, in my imagination, is enough to wake me up. It's enough to get me out of bed and want to sit in the dark on my own. That's quite intense that, isn't it?

**Chloe**   Do you think you might be depressed?

**Nick**   Depressed? Why would you say that?

**Chloe**   It's a sign, isn't it, not being able to sleep.

**Nick**   Having bad dreams? Everyone has bad dreams.

**Chloe**   The dream's just detail.

**Nick**   I really don't think I'm depressed.

**Chloe**   What if we decorated?

**Nick**   *Decorated*? Where did that come from?

**Chloe**   I read this thing about stasis. Stasis is like the environment where depression and lethargy and, and a lack of enthusiasm fester. It's a psychological thing. Change is the first step towards fighting it.

**Nick**   Where the hell did you read that?

**Chloe**   Online.

**Nick**   We're not in stasis.

**Chloe**   We haven't decorated since we moved in.

**Nick**   That's not true. I put up those Batman posters and then you took them down. That's like *two* redecorations.

**Chloe**   We moved in after university. It's like we're still living in a student house and it's nothing to be proud of, Nick. At our age, it's really not. We should be more like Yani and Tim. They bought a house and they're not depressed.

**Nick**   Buying houses . . . We're not Tories, Chloe.

**Chloe**   You can't just call anyone who shows any ambition in life a Tory.

**Nick**   You used to.

**Chloe**   I'm starting to look back and maybe the really hard-working kids at uni weren't the dickheads we said they were. Maybe they were just smart. I don't know how much we've got to show for where we are in our lives.

**Nick**   You're getting all this from one article?

**Chloe**   No, Nick. Loads of articles. It's what normal people talk about. Moving, decorating . . .

**Nick**   Going running at five in the morning?

**Chloe**   Yes, exercise as well.

**Nick**   Look, you can't let all that kind of nonsense get into your head. It's noise, is all it is. You work with a lot of people who are older than you. That can have an effect on your brain. You start to think like them.

**Chloe**   Like you working with kids, you mean?

**Nick**   That's different. I don't listen to the kids. Besides, they hate me.

**Chloe**   They don't hate you. What about Year 8 and the card they got you on your birthday?

**Nick**   No one likes Year 8. Do you know how embarrassing that was? In front of Year 9 as well. Now that's a year to impress.

**Chloe**   Nick, I'm worried that we're not normal. I'm worried that we should have moved on from here. And maybe you're worried too. Maybe that's why you're depressed.

**Nick**   I'm not depressed.

**Chloe**   But you're up at half five eating cereal in the dark. So there's something. Isn't there?

**Three**

*Later that morning.*

*The staffroom.*

**Jo**   Here, look at this.

**Nick**   What is it?

**Jo**   Marking from last night. A key lesson for you, Nick. What does it look like?

**Nick**   Looks like he's got it all wrong.

**Jo**   Exactly. But see, he does pretty solid in class. Why do you reckon his homework's shit?

**Nick**   I don't know. Spends no time on it? Rushes it in the morning?

**Jo**   No. The opposite. He's sat at that kitchen table for hours. Look at his handwriting. Better than in class. You know why his handwriting's so good but the work's so crap?

**Nick**   I give up.

**Jo**   Parents. Cheating fucking parents.

**Nick**   Really?

**Jo**   You can tell when the parents have had a crack at helping. They're always worse than the kids.

**Nick**   How does that work?

**Jo**   Well think about it. Your kid's here day after day learning real bloody technical stuff, maybe you might want to step away from the coursework when all you do is dick around on Facebook all day.

**Nick**   Right, yeah. That's good to know. To keep an eye out for.

**Jo**   Don't blame the kid. Never blame the kid. It's the arrogance of adults.

**Nick**   Arrogance of adults, I like that.

**Jo**   Course, you can't say anything. Parents are sacred. If it wasn't for the parents then we wouldn't have a job. And don't they know it. Had one the other day ask me if I could recommend somewhere they could take their kids on the weekend. I said yeah, *home*. Like, parent them yourselves for two days a week.

**Nick**   I can't believe the adult got all these fucking answers wrong.

**Jo**   Mrs Richardson just heard you say *fucking*.

**Nick**   Ah really? I get funny about old people hearing me swear. Like I'm letting them down.

**Jo**   How's it letting them down?

**Nick**   It's like they've given me this language and all I'm doing is using it to say fuck.

**Jo**   You don't think they said fuck?

**Nick**   Yeah but they said it like *fuck the Nazis, fuck . . . polio*. What are we saying fuck to? Wifi?

**Jo**   I'm sure she hears worse. She's got Year 10 biology.

**Nick**   Year 10 are savages. I don't know what it is about them. Maybe she can block it out. Like she has a filter. I don't have a filter. I soak it up like a sponge. No wonder Chloe thinks I'm depressed.

**Jo**   You're not depressed. You're stressed.

**Nick**   You think?

**Jo**   Textbook, mate.

**Nick**  Oh phew, I thought there was something . . . you know, serious.

**Jo**  Stress is serious. It could kill you, Nick.

**Nick**  Stress could kill me? Like on its own or with something else?

**Jo**  On its own.

**Nick**  Well that's pretty stressful. You think I'm more stressed than normal?

**Jo**  I don't know. You tell me.

**Nick**  I'm not sleeping well but that's it. I keep getting this dream where . . . Well, whatever. It's just a dream.

**Jo**  Just a dream? Never *just* a dream, Nick.

**Nick**  What do you mean?

**Jo**  Dreams are important. Dreams are signals.

**Nick**  Signals?

**Jo**  They're your subconscious trying to tell you something.

**Nick**  You really believe that?

**Jo**  It's serious stuff. Your subconscious is the point your body and your head connect. You're just at one end of the line. What happens in the dream?

**Nick**  I don't know if I want to say.

**Jo**  It's a sex dream?

**Nick**  No. What's everyone . . . No, it's . . . Look, it doesn't matter what it's about. If my mind's trying to tell me something then why doesn't it say? It says when I need to sit down or eat or something.

**Jo**  This isn't like needing to eat. I'm talking about deep psychological things.

**Nick** I don't know if I want to listen to deep psychological things.

**Jo** Ignore it if you want, but that's a risk you're deciding to take.

**Nick** Oh no. It'd be a risk to . . . you know. I don't take risks. I like to play it safe.

**Jo** But you're taking a risk thinking you know what safe is. Safe isn't always an option.

**Nick** You think?

**Jo** Think of a cat in the middle of a busy road. There's no safe way of getting to either side with all these cars like zooming past in both directions. The cat's got to be aware of the risks. But it's also got to move, it's got to get through the traffic to, to /

**Nick** / But what if the cat just stays there, waiting for all the traffic to pass?

**Jo** A cat sat in the road is taking a bigger risk than a cat running across it. Think about it.

**Nick** I don't know. Life can't be that intense, even for cats.

**Jo** Well it's what happened this morning and I went bang right over it.

**Nick** Over what?

**Jo** The cat.

**Nick** This actually happened? I thought it was just a metaphor. Holy shit. Poor cat.

**Jo** Poor cat? It made its choices.

**Nick** What did you do?

**Jo** What do you mean?

**Nick** You didn't stop?

**Jo**   Where could I stop? I was on my way to the school.

**Nick**   How old was it?

**Jo**   It was definitely an older cat. Adult to mature.

**Nick**   Oh. Well that's something. I mean, don't get me wrong – kill nothing. But it's a cat that's lived its life.

*Beat.*

Nightingale still isn't in. That means I've got her lunch club then.

**Jo**   Didn't you hear? It's cancer.

**Nick**   Cancer . . . What can you do with cancer?

**Jo**   You can hope.

**Nick**   That's true.

**Jo**   But she is dying.

**Nick**   Well. It is cancer.

**Jo**   There's a card going round.

**Nick**   Well, yeah.

**Jo**   Yeah, but /

**Nick**   / I should sign it.

**Jo**   Course you should sign it. But see the /

**Nick**   / I really need to make sure. You can't not sign these things.

**Jo**   You're going to sign it, Nick. Will you let me finish? What I was saying is that this card has got Jesus on it.

**Nick**   Jesus Christ?

**Jo**   What other Jesus is there? It's not like saying Paul. Paul who? Paul McKenna? Paul McCartney? Jesus is Jesus. Like Prince.

**Nick**    Is Prince his name or is it his title?

**Jo**    It's a name. Where's he going to be prince of? Minnesota?

**Nick**    Why Minnesota?

**Jo**    It's where he's from.

**Nick**    How do you know that?

**Jo**    I like Purple Rain. Will you let me tell you about this fucking card?

**Nick**    Ok.

**Jo**    Well it's all *with sympathy* and that, like she's already dead, and there on the front it's got Jesus on it. And I'm like *look isn't this a bit tasteless?*

**Nick**    Why would it be tasteless? Is she Jewish?

**Jo**    No, she's not Jewish. I don't know what she is. But she's not going to appreciate Jesus on a card.

**Nick**    Why not?

**Jo**    Because it's cancer, Nick. And a card like that is a sign. It's a sign that if you believe in Jesus then you must also believe in a reason for her cancer.

**Nick**    So you're saying because there's Jesus on the front it's implying that God gave Mrs Nightingale cancer on purpose?

**Jo**    Exactly.

**Nick**    And what did they say?

**Jo**    They asked me if I wanted to get my own card.

**Nick**    And are you?

**Jo**    Course not. I wasn't telling you because I want to do anything about it. Plus, Jesus came back. She won't. He's the last person you want on a card.

**Nick**    Mrs Nightingale . . . You never think it's going to be you, do you?

**Jo**    It's what life does to you. You think you've got it all making sense and then . . . *boom*.

**Nick**    Boom?

**Jo**    Boom.

## Four

*That lunchtime.*

*Mrs Nightingale's class.*

**Jessica** *enters.*

**Nick**    Oh hey, yeah. Come in. I'm covering today.

*Beat.*

Does it normally start late?

**Jessica**    No.

**Nick**    Oh.

*Beat.*

What's your name?

**Jessica**    Jessica Havens.

**Nick**    I don't recognise you. What form are you in?

**Jessica**    10D.

**Nick**    Oh Mr Davies.

**Jessica**    Yeah.

**Nick**    Sorry. I'm still learning names. I'm new. Well, last term. End of the term before last. That's not new at all, really, is it?

*Beat.*

We'll give it five minutes. Just waiting for the others.

**Jessica**   It's just me.

**Nick**   What?

**Jessica**   It's just me. That comes.

**Nick**   Why's it only you?

**Jessica**   I don't know. It's only ever me that does maths club.

**Nick**   Since when?

**Jessica**   Dunno.

**Nick**   How long's *dunno*? Weeks? Months?

**Jessica**   Months.

**Nick**   Months?

**Jessica**   Yeah.

**Nick**   Mrs Nightingale just does this for you? Every day? For months?

**Jessica**   Yeah.

**Nick**   Why?

**Jessica**   To get better at maths.

**Nick**   But it's lunchtime.

**Jessica**   I know.

**Nick**   No one else cares about getting better at maths at lunchtime. Are you bad at maths?

**Jessica**   No.

**Nick**   Then why are you here?

**Jessica**   I enjoy it.

*Beat.*

**Nick**   Good. That's good.

**Jessica**   Is Mrs Nightingale coming back?

**Nick**   No. I don't know. Yes. I hope so. Didn't you hear? She's got . . . ill. She's ill.

**Jessica**   Oh.

**Nick**   Yeah.

**Jessica**   Should I go?

**Nick**   What?

**Jessica**   Should I go? If there's no maths?

**Nick**   Well what would you do? About your . . .

**Jessica**   I don't know.

**Nick**   They'd be no maths club.

**Jessica**   Yeah.

**Nick**   I mean I don't want to just leave you. I suppose
I can speak to Mr Boyd. Maybe someone else can keep it
a regular thing.

**Jessica**   Ok.

**Nick**   But there's no reason why I can't do today. For the
next week even. If they need me to. Until someone else can
do it.

**Jessica**   Thank you.

**Nick**   What?

**Jessica**   Nothing. I just said thank you.

**Nick**   Oh. You're welcome.


**Five**

*That afternoon.*

*In class.*

**Nick**   Mrs Nichols is off today so . . . Now that's not . . .
Hey, can we quieten down? Now that's not licence to do
nothing, ok? Has anybody not brought their textbooks?

Natalie, this is like the third lesson I've had you in this week and you've never had the right books. What's going on? Do you not have a timetable?

Peter, can you sit down, please? Why are you so excited?

Karen, stop chewing that.

Peter, Karen can stop chewing it on her own, thank you.

Everyone quieten down. I'm not sure where you've got with this so let's start at the beginning. Don't moan, this is revision. Ok so, *Tale of Two Cities*. Who wants to read?

No one. Ok. I'll read.

*It was the best of times, it was the worst of times. It was the age of wisdom, it was the age of foolishness. It was the epoch of belief, it was the epoch of incredulity. It was the season of Light, it was the season of Darkness. It was the spring of hope, it was the winter of despair. We had everything before us, we had nothing before us.*

Um, before we carry on. Can anyone tell me what this means?

It conveys the novel's central tensions, the themes. We have love and family on the one side and we have war and hatred and violence on the other. Dickens uses an anaphora . . . Can anyone tell me what an anaphora is?

Ok, so write this down. An anaphora is the repetition of a phrase at the beginning of consecutive clauses. *It was the age . . . it was the age, it was the epoch . . . it was the epoch . . .* Etcetera.

Dickens is suggesting that good and evil and light and dark stand equally matched. They're opposites, but they're connected, yeah? As ideas. Think of it like a road that goes North, it also goes South. The road itself points in both directions. It's all about which way you're facing. Can anyone think of any examples of their own?

What's that, Tim?

Awake and dreaming. Um, but I mean would, would you say that they are . . . Dreams are just . . . They're not part of the same thing. They're not connected. Are they? *Are they?*

*Beat.*

Hey so anyway, you all get the point. Let's move on to the . . . the next bit. Uh . . . How about you just read by yourselves in your heads? Ok?

In your head, Peter.

## Six

*Later that afternoon.*

**Mr Boyd***'s office.*

**Nick**    But I know nothing of physics.

**Mr Boyd**    You know what it means to sit down. You know light and dark. These are fundamental physical things.

**Nick**    There's more to it than that.

**Mr Boyd**    But you can't say you know nothing. You're resourceful.

**Nick**    I'm completely lost with the sciences.

**Mr Boyd**    That's ok. No one's an expert.

**Nick**    But we're teachers. I think we're meant to be experts.

**Mr Boyd**    We have books and computers /

**Nick**    / If I'm covering for Mrs Patel then /

**Mr Boyd**    / and videos.

**Nick**    Then the students are going to know more than I do.

**Mr Boyd**    They'll be able to help you.

**Nick**    Help me teach them? How would that work? I don't know if I can teach a lesson I know nothing about.

**Mr Boyd**   You cover for maths. You cover for English.

**Nick**   And that's exactly what I wanted to talk to you about. I feel like I'm drowning in other people's classes. I haven't had a day of just my own classes in months.

**Mr Boyd**   History will still be there. Don't you worry about that. We're going through a very awkward period right now, Nick. A tragic and awkward . . . a *tragically* awkward period. Mrs Nightingale /

**Nick**   / No, I know. I'm not trying to say /

**Mr Boyd**   / Mrs Nightingale has *cancer*.

**Nick**   I know she does. No, I know. I'm sorry. I don't mean to be . . . I suppose I'm just a little anxious at the moment, Mr Boyd. Does that make sense? I'm stressed.

**Mr Boyd**   Oh you're not stressed.

**Nick**   I'm not? Do you think I'm depressed?

**Mr Boyd**   No, you're not depressed either.

**Nick**   Then what's wrong with me?

**Mr Boyd**   You're modern. You're a very modern man, Nick.

**Nick**   Thank you . . .?

**Mr Boyd**   And it's no good for you. You never have a break from it. Constant noise. Look at your phone there. Buzzing away.

**Nick**   My phone's off.

**Mr Boyd**   And so suspicious. You never trust a thing anyone says.

**Nick**   I don't think that's true.

**Mr Boyd**   Now don't get me wrong, you've got to be worried. Don't be ignorant – there's so much to worry about. Violence. Catastrophe. I'm talking about the world. Not just your own life.

**Nick**    No, well, that's what I thought.

**Mr Boyd**    A little anxiety is good for you. It shows you're paying attention. Keeps you on your toes.

**Nick**    But too much of it can kill you.

**Mr Boyd**    I don't think that's right. I've never heard of anyone dying of worry. Now you've only been here a few months. You'll settle in.

**Nick**    I think there's more to it than just settling in, Mr Boyd.

**Mr Boyd**    Teaching brings with it a unique set of challenges.

**Nick**    I know.

**Mr Boyd**    It can be a lot to deal with. Not everybody can teach. You've got here and that's a lot more than most.

**Nick**    I think my, my anxiety is manifesting itself in my thoughts. Pictures. And it makes me worry about my job. I know that how I feel about myself must be having some effect on the pupils. Like they can smell my doubt or something.

**Mr Boyd**    Children don't know what they can smell.

**Nick**    Maybe it's that I don't know where I should be heading.

**Mr Boyd**    How old are you?

**Nick**    I'm twenty-eight.

**Mr Boyd**    Well.

**Nick**    Well what?

**Mr Boyd**    Well that's where you're going wrong. You're twenty-eight. You've probably got to where you're going. You don't feel like you're getting anywhere because you're already there.

**Nick**   But that's not comforting at all. I don't think I could live with myself if I died without achieving more.

**Mr Boyd**   So is that it, Nick? You're scared of dying?

**Nick**   Of course I am. Who isn't? Mr Boyd, I'm not sleeping very well.

**Mr Boyd**   Oh.

**Nick**   *Oh*? Why *oh*?

**Mr Boyd**   You said you were stressed but you didn't mention sleep. Sleep's important. Don't you know you need to sleep?

**Nick**   It's not . . . I mean, yes of course I do. It's not out of choice.

**Mr Boyd**   Sleep is vital for a healthy brain.

**Nick**   I've been starting to have very strange dreams.

**Mr Boyd**   All dreams are strange, Nick. They're meant to be strange. Very strange.

**Nick**   Not like these dreams.

**Mr Boyd**   What happens in them?

**Nick**   I don't know if I want to /

**Mr Boyd**   / Yes I remember my first years in the teaching game. Geography, it was. I was torn to bits day after day. You'll soon get used to it. That mild panic. You get tuned out of it. It'll hum like a fridge and you don't hear the hum of fridges, do you?

**Nick**   I don't know if I can do that. Mr Boyd, I /

**Mr Boyd**   / Yes you can, Nick. Yes you can.

**Nick**   Mr Boyd, I dream about a bomb under the school. I dream that there's this bomb and every night it explodes. I don't want it in my head and I can't ignore it like you say I should.

*Beat.*

It probably means nothing, though. It means nothing, right?
It's just like a . . . I mean, you know what it's like.
Imaginations. Strange dreams. You know?

*Beat.*

Mr Boyd?

**Mr Boyd**    Funny.

**Nick**    What's funny? How's that funny?

**Mr Boyd**    Yes, very clever. Very sharp.

**Nick**    I don't understand.

**Mr Boyd**    *I've been having dreams. The bomb, the bomb.* Yes, fair
play. I didn't see it coming at all. You pranked me. One nil.

**Nick**    Mr Boyd, it isn't a prank. I'm being serious.

**Mr Boyd**    It's a funny joke, Nick. But don't milk it.

**Nick**    I'm not milking anything. I don't know what you're
talking about.

**Mr Boyd**    You're teasing me about the bomb. The old one
up on the Brink.

**Nick**    I was talking about my dream, Mr Boyd. There's a
bomb? Like an actual, real bomb? It was the Brink in my
dream. They said it was the Brink. Why am I dreaming
about a, a . . .?

**Mr Boyd**    You didn't know?

**Nick**    No!

*Beat.*

**Mr Boyd**    I did wonder who would've approved of your
knowing. You don't seem their type. And I appear to have
just let the little bugger slip out, haven't I? Oh dear.

**Nick**   Are you really telling me there's a bomb up on the playing fields, Mr Boyd?

**Mr Boyd**   Oh it's all perfectly safe. It's an old deactivated World War Two bomb. Left from the Blitz. Couldn't move it. Too big, it was. Covered in concrete now. You'll have to promise me to keep it to yourself. This gets out and people would overreact.

**Nick**   They'd overreact? Mr Boyd, this is madness. A bomb at the school and you're keeping it a secret? Why would someone build a school on top of a bomb?

**Mr Boyd**   Well, they didn't. The fields were never meant to be part of the school.

**Nick**   Doesn't it seem bizarre to you that this is exactly what I've been dreaming of? This exact thing? Except in my dream it explodes.

**Mr Boyd**   Now, Nick . . .

**Nick**   What if it's . . . a vision? What if my dreams are a sign that it'll explode?

**Mr Boyd**   It's been down there for so long. Who says it's going to explode?

**Nick**   Because it's meant to. That's its job.

**Mr Boyd**   I don't think we should get too excited.

**Nick**   Has anybody even checked it recently? I mean, if it's under concrete then we've got no idea what condition it's in. It could explode any second. I don't like the idea of not knowing, Mr Boyd. Don't you think we should do something about it?

**Mr Boyd**   You *are* doing something. You're making a rational decision not to alarm people.

**Nick**   All this, I mean, it's a lot to take in.

**Mr Boyd**    But not impossible. You can take this in, Nick. Concentrate and it will go in.

**Nick**    How can I teach on top of a bomb?

**Mr Boyd**    You'll find a way. You'll have to. We need you at your best. Education is a fragile, dear vocation. You are the world to many children here. Their very lives are in your hands.


**Seven**

*That afternoon.*

*The school fields.*

**Students** *are running.*

**Three**    Keep up, sir.

**Two**    Come on, sir.

**Nick**    I'm coming. Just keep going.

**Three**    We don't know where to go, sir.

**Nick**    Past the fence.

**One**    Where?

**Nick**    Past the . . .

*He catches up with them.*

I said past the fence. Let's have two minutes then. Catch our breath.

**Two**    We don't need to catch our breath, sir.

**One**    We want to keep going.

**Nick**    No, no. Breaths are important. Don't you learn anything in biology? It's . . . I don't know. It's for your muscles or whatever.

**Three**    We're meant to be running, sir.

**Nick**    We are running. We're just recapping on what we've run so far.

**Two**    We don't normally have to wait for the teacher.

**Nick**    Yeah well it's not my lesson.

**Two**    But you're an adult. Shouldn't be this out of puff, sir.

**Three**    Are you dying, sir?

**Nick**    Of course I'm not dying.

**Three**    Don't you worry though?

**Nick**    About what?

**Three**    Dying, sir.

**Nick**    I'm not . . . I'm not dying.

**One**    You were sweating putting your trainers on.

**Nick**    That doesn't mean I'm dying. That's just a problem with salt.

**One**    Must be a worry though, mustn't it? Not being able to run.

**Nick**    I can run if I want to.

**Two**    Is it scary being old, sir?

**Nick**    I don't know. What kind of question is that?

**Two**    Scares me.

**Three**    Yeah, scares me too.

**Nick**    I'm not as old as you think I am. How old do you think I am?

**Two**    Twenty-eight.

**Nick**    That's . . . Well, it's not that old, is it?

**Three**    Is Mrs Nightingale still alive, sir?

**Nick**   Yes, she's still alive. How'd you get from my age to Mrs Nightingale? Twenty-eight is still young. Not as young as you, granted.

**Three**   I was just wondering how she's doing, sir.

**Nick**   She's ok, I think. I don't know. It's cancer. You never know with cancer, do you? Look. Come on. Let's go back. We'll go back the way we came and, I don't know, round the cricket square. That's enough for the day.

**Two**   Oh but, sir, we've only just got to the Brink.

**Nick**   I thought that was the Brink over there. The ledge in the grass.

**One**   Brink curves round, sir.

**Nick**   We're on the Brink now? That's . . . It comes this far? This is a slant, not a brink . . . Why would you call . . .

**Three**   Are you alright, sir?

**Nick**   You wouldn't have any idea just by looking at it.

**One**   Look at what?

**Nick**   The ground.

**Two**   Sir?

**Nick**   Does it feel warm to you? It feels warm. On your hands. Burning under the surface. How can he say that it's safe?

**Three**   What's safe?

**Nick**   Exactly. What is safe? We don't know. Don't you feel it? Can't you feel it under your feet?

**One**   Feel what, sir?

**Nick**   Under the ground here, right directly under us is a . . . a . . .

**Two**   A what?

*Beat.*

**Three**    What are you talking about, sir?

**Nick**    Nothing. No, nothing. Let's . . . let's go back. Run back that way.

**One**    But, sir, we came from that way.

**Nick**    Yeah well think of it as revision. Look at the time. Don't want to be late for your next class. Come on. You lot run on, I'll catch you up.

*The students run on.*

**Nick** *has a moment on the Brink.*

*He hears a sound.*

Hello?

**Mr Boyd** (*off*)    It's me, Nick.

**Nick**    Mr Boyd. What . . .

**Mr Boyd** *walks up.*

**Nick**    What are you doing out on the . . .?

**Mr Boyd**    I saw you come up here. With your class.

**Nick**    I didn't realise the Brink came out this far. Did you follow us?

**Mr Boyd**    You wanted to tell them.

**Nick**    Of course I wanted to. Were you . . . were you making sure that I didn't?

**Mr Boyd**    No. Of course not. I didn't need to anyway. You thought better of it.

**Nick**    I couldn't do it. I couldn't find the words.

**Mr Boyd**    You felt a responsibility. A responsibility to calm.

**Nick**    It's more that I wouldn't know where to start.

**Mr Boyd**   Even after you left my office I still wasn't sure whether or not you were joking with me. And I realised that you couldn't have been. You don't have an ounce of humour in your body, Nick. And that worried me. Of course, you're going to have to tell me who told you about the bomb.

**Nick**   I'm being serious, Mr Boyd. I promise you that nobody told me. It was just these dreams. These dreams that I made up in my in my own head and they happen to be true. Can't you see how this is more worrying for me? I mean, I wonder if I need to see someone.

**Mr Boyd**   No. Never. You can never do that, Nick. We have had to keep the tightest of lids on this. And we've done a very good job. And so now are you. You're now another hand holding up this great weight. You're part of something important. Could you imagine the chaos if it got out?

**Nick**   But I thought you said it was safe.

**Mr Boyd**   Let's not be naïve, Nick. It's not the bomb itself that I'm worried about. Enough damage can be done with the word alone. You say *bomb* and it paints a terrible picture. They're children. They have precious, tender minds and a head can break only once.

**Nick**   But what about the parents? A carefully worded letter might /

**Mr Boyd**   / The parents would be even worse. Parents expect schools to be a refuge from today, a vestige for their own nostalgia. School to your parent is where custard is still pink and dinner ladies are still obese in a fun way. These parents had no other way into the world and can't imagine any other way for their children. We tell them about the bomb today and this school will never be the same. And you don't want that, Nick. It would work out very poorly for you.

**Nick**   Are you threatening me, Mr Boyd?

**Mr Boyd**   No. Of course not. No. Not at all.

**Nick**   Oh that's a relief.

**Mr Boyd**   But I am talking about the delivery and provision of education for young people in the surrounding area. Which I know you care very much about.

**Nick**   Of course I do.

**Mr Boyd**   And so if something was to come out that would disrupt our students' progress . . . A rumour about a bomb, perhaps, after all this time keeping it a tip-top secret . . . Well, it wouldn't take an expert to work out whose fault that would be. And if that was to happen, well never mind what other people would think, we both know that you'd just have to kill yourself.

**Nick**   *Kill* myself? Did you say kill myself?

**Mr Boyd**   No, I said that we both know that you just wouldn't be able to live with yourself.

**Nick**   Right. Because I thought you said /

**Mr Boyd**   / I am trusting you here, and I know that you are trusting yourself, to do the right thing.

*He starts walking away.*

**Nick**   So what should I do about the dreams then, Mr Boyd?

*Beat.*

Mr Boyd?

## Part Two

### One

*The present. Night time.*

**Nick** *is on the school field.*

**Nick**   So I'm stood there and the school starts to sag out of this blast hole like a punctured bladder. A punctured bladder on fire. I can't tell you how much fire there is. And I realise that the smell isn't coming from the brick or the softening glass, but from the bodies. And they're popping and crackling and going off in all sorts of colours like fireworks. And those that can't scream or cry are just making the others scream and cry even more. And I don't know what's worse – the dead or the dying. Some of them are shouting *Mum* and *Dad* but they're not really calling for their mums or dads at all – they're just begging the air. Then out of nowhere someone says *can you help me, sir?* And I can't. I know that I *can't*.

### Two

*Earlier.*

*The morning.*

*In the car.*

**Chloe**   Can you close your window?

**Nick**   I like it open. I don't like the . . .

**Chloe**   It stinks.

**Nick**   What stinks? Who stinks?

**Chloe**   Outside.

**Nick**    Outside? How can you say outside stinks? It's outside. There's so much of it. It can't all stink.

**Chloe**    There's a general smell. It must have been the park.

**Nick**    The park's the park. It's the city that stinks. Pollution and, and . . . The park is life. Kids playing up trees. Old men playing chess.

**Chloe**    Old men don't play chess in the park, Nick. Old men wank in the park.

**Nick**    Not in the daytime. At least not where you can see.

*Beat.*

No alarm clocks in the park. No one telling you what to do. No stress, no secrets. It's peace. It's paradise, Chloe.

**Chloe**    Are you drunk? Have you started drinking in the morning? Shit.

**Nick**    No. I'm not . . . I'm not drinking in the morning. I'm just . . . Hey, maybe I'm paying attention to the world for the first time in my life.

*Pause.*

**Chloe**    I was talking to Gina yesterday about your dreams and she /

**Nick**    / Hang on. Gina?

**Chloe**    And she said that bad dreams about the workplace often suggest anxiety about the future.

**Nick**    Why were you talking to Gina about my dreams?

**Chloe**    Because she knows.

**Nick**    What does she know?

**Chloe**    She studies what dreams mean. It's her thing. She's very good.

**Nick**   Don't talk to Gina about my dreams, Chloe. Don't talk to anyone about my dreams. Bloody hell.

**Chloe**   I was just asking for advice.

**Nick**   Well, you shouldn't.

**Chloe**   I can't do anything right.

**Nick**   I don't want it getting out. I don't want people knowing about my dreams. Not before I've worked out what I should do about them.

**Chloe**   You haven't even told me what happens in them so she couldn't /

**Nick**   / Yeah well it's a good job I haven't otherwise it would've been broadcast all over the bloody BBC by now. And then I'd be in the shit.

**Chloe**   Why would you be in the shit?

*Beat.*

**Nick**   Telling Gina. I thought yoga was her thing, not dreams.

**Chloe**   You can have more than one thing, Nick.

**Nick**   *Bullshit* is her thing. It all comes under the umbrella of . . . bloody horseshit.

**Chloe**   Well pick one. Horseshit and bullshit are two different things. The clues are in the names. Comes from different fucking animals.

*Beat.*

You can't just expect me to ignore it when you tell me you're having horrible dreams, Nick. You were petrified the other day. If you're going through something then you need to let me in. Or if not me then someone who can help you.

**Nick**   Like who?

**Chloe**    There are people there . . . Specialists . . . Someone who can help you understand what it is.

**Nick**    Now, hang on.

**Chloe**    You shouldn't have to keep this a secret. You could even get a doctor to write a note to the school as well. Explaining what these dreams are and why you need more support. This is a big thing, Nick.

*Beat.*

Nick? Are you listening?

**Nick**    Yeah.

**Chloe**    There are people who would want to know.

**Nick**    No, I . . .

**Chloe**    Why don't I book you an appointment with the doctor at lunch?

**Nick**    They're . . . They've stopped.

**Chloe**    What?

**Nick**    They've stopped. The dreams have stopped.

**Chloe**    They've stopped?

**Nick**    Yeah. I don't know what it was. But they're gone.

**Chloe**    Just like that?

**Nick**    Just like that. So strange. Scary, you know. But they've stopped and I feel much better. In myself. I don't need to see a doctor.

**Chloe**    Why didn't you say?

**Nick**    I was embarrassed. I'm sorry.

**Chloe**    So you're not depressed?

**Nick**    No. Not any more than anyone else anyway. That's why I didn't want you talking to Gina. I didn't want you to panic. I'm sorry.

*Pause.*

**Chloe**    Since when?

**Nick**    Since when what?

**Chloe**    Since when did they stop?

**Nick**    I don't know. I slept pretty well last night.

**Chloe**    Last night could just be a one-off.

**Nick**    Bloody hell. Sounds like you want me to be having them, Chloe. Aren't you happy they've stopped? Isn't it good news?

**Chloe**    Yeah. No, of course.

**Nick**    I woke up this morning and I feel really, massively improved.

**Chloe**    Good.

*Beat.*

It just seems /

**Nick**    / What?

**Chloe**    It just seems a little quick. I mean, even if the dreams have stopped that doesn't mean that a sense of stasis isn't /

**Nick**    / You keep saying stasis. Stasis isn't a thing. And even if it was a thing then maybe it isn't a bad idea. Maybe I don't want change. Maybe I want everything to be fine and safe and just like it's meant to be. Nothing different, no surprises. You start uprooting and you don't know what you're going to uncover. Leave it be. Leave everything be.

*Silence.*

**Chloe**   It's Martin's tonight, remember.

**Nick**   Martin's what?

**Chloe**   We're going to Martin's. For dinner.

**Nick**   Oh shit. No. I forgot.

**Chloe**   Nick. You promised.

**Nick**   Ok. It's fine.

**Chloe**   *Fine*? Bloody hell, it's not asking for a lot is it?

**Nick**   I said it was fine. Fine is a good thing.

**Chloe**   Good is good. Fine is just fine.

**Nick**   Fine is accepting the fact of the event.

**Chloe**   I'm just asking you to sit and eat the food someone else has made you and be generally receptive to conversation. I mean, you spend all day trying to not tell kids to fuck off, maybe you can manage to be polite to my boss for a few hours, if you, like, really concentrate?

**Nick**   I'll try my best.

**Chloe**   It's nice he's invited us. This doesn't happen all the time you know. It's a sign that he's got plans and maybe I'm a part of them. Please, for my sake, behave.

**Nick**   I will.

**Chloe**   Thank you.

*Beat.*

Will you remember to wear a good shirt?

**Nick**   Isn't this a good shirt?

**Chloe**   No. Where am I parking?

**Nick**   Turn in here. In front of the buses. Fuck them.

**Three**

*Later that morning.*

*The staffroom.*

**Jo**    . . . and so I get this feeling /

**Nick**    / Jo.

**Jo**    I'm stood there and I'm, like /

**Nick**    / Jo, I'm a bit worried about /

**Jo**    / No, let me finish. See it must've been /

**Nick**    / No, I need to talk to you. Before the bell.

**Jo**    After this. After. You need to hear it.

**Nick**    But, Jo /

**Jo**    / So it must've been the fish because it went through me like a fucking motorway. And so I'm there on the toilet. But the smell is so bad it's making me gag. And Thom's at the door, banging, and this is how I know it's the fish, because he needs to throw up too. So he's banging at the door and I'm like, *no you can't come in and see me shitting like this* because we might've got to that biblical stage in our relationship but we're still definitely New Testament, not Old Testament. But this is an emergency and before he knocks the door down I unlatch it and in he comes. Thankfully it's had a different effect on him so he's needing to throw it all up. So while I'm sat on the toilet he's in the bath, vomiting down the plughole. But that's not all. The smell from me is making him throw up even more and what with watching him throw up, my gagging starts to turn into full on retching and I'm having to lean over the sink and throw up in there while the world falls out of my arse. Watching me throw up is making him throw up more too so the pair of us are there throwing our guts up and you can imagine the mess. The bathroom starts off looking like a Pollock painting but ends up looking more like a Rothko.

*Beat.*

Oh and then he starts shitting too.

*Beat.*

What did you want to talk about?

**Nick**   I . . . I need your help with something, Jo. Something serious that I'm not even meant to talk about. You see /

*She notices something.*

**Jo**   / What the fuck is this?

**Nick**   What?

**Jo**   The rota. Why the fuck am I down doing your second period? And *why* am I covering your whole afternoon? Fucking hell, Nick.

**Nick**   What? Let me see.

**Jo**   I was trying to keep that free. You know how much marking I've got to do.

**Nick**   I'm not on the rota at all. I've been unrotaed.

**Jo**   I'm going to have to do my marking at home now. I'm going to have to work late and that's another night Thom and I can't have sex. Are you trying to ruin my life?

**Nick**   Jo, this is it. This is what I wanted to talk to you about. I know too much.

**Jo**   What?

**Nick**   Mr Boyd thinks I'm going to tell the pupils. He's keeping me out of the class so I can't tell anyone.

**Jo**   Tell anyone what? I've got no idea what you're going on about.

**Nick**   It's a secret that he's keeping from us, from the pupils. The school isn't safe. Mr Boyd told me himself. He admitted it. Right underneath the ground there's a . . . Why are you smirking? Jo, this isn't funny.

**Jo**    I wouldn't listen to Boyd.

**Nick**    Why not?

**Jo**    He's been all over the place since Ashbury High closed.

**Nick**    Ashbury High – the, the asbestos school?

**Jo**    Yeah and Boyd's doing everything he can to get this place closed down too. He had Daniels chasing the birds on the roof because he was sure they were carrying impetigo.

**Nick**    Why would Boyd want the school closed down?

**Jo**    Think about it. They tear down these old schools and filter the kids off into bigger academies. The kind of academies that Boyd wants to work in. He's seeing all these heads with super-budgets and Apple computers and shit and look at us, we have to photocopy pages out of textbooks. He can't wait to get out. Except of course he can't quit because it would look bad on his CV. However, if the school happened to close . . .

**Nick**    Then he can move on with his reputation intact.

**Jo**    Even better, he'll look like the hero that saved all these kids from an unsafe school. Clever, no? So just ignore whatever he's told you. At some point he's going to have to prove it and when he can't, he'll just end up looking like even more of an idiot.

**Nick**    It can't be that simple.

**Jo**    It is.

**Nick**    But there's a bomb, Jo. There's an actual bomb. Under the school. Left from the Second World War underneath the playing fields.

*Beat.*

**Jo**    So that's how he'll do it.

**Nick**    Do what?

**Jo**　They'd have to excavate the whole area. That kind of work would be too expensive. Easier to shut the whole place down.

**Nick**　But, Jo, he didn't tell me that the bomb was there. I found out and he admitted it because he thought I already knew.

**Jo**　Who told you then?

**Nick**　No one. See, it all matches perfectly with these dreams I've been having, where every night a bomb goes off and kills everyone.

**Jo**　And so you told Boyd you were having these dreams and he just said *well yeah funny you should say that.*

**Nick**　Kind of. Yeah.

**Jo**　Jesus.

*Beat.*

How do I know Boyd isn't just using you to spook up more teachers? Get them behind this bomb idea and then *make* him close the school?

**Nick**　Because he told me to keep it a secret. He threatened me.

**Jo**　He threatened you?

**Nick**　Well, he didn't quite threaten me but there was definitely an element of displeasure in, in the idea of me spreading the information. I'm only telling you because I'm going to fucking burst and I know you'd know what to do about it. I didn't even tell Chloe. I told her the dreams have stopped. I lied to her. I never lie to Chloe. Except maybe about how many carbohydrates I eat at lunch.

**Jo**　It doesn't make any sense.

**Nick**　None of it makes any sense and, and stuff like this, stuff like taking me off the rota, is only making me even more sure that this is some serious shit. I mean, if Boyd really is trying to get the school closed down then why's he going to all this effort to silence me?

**Jo**   Maybe he's waiting for a particular job. He's got his eye on something really specific, and you've found out too soon.

**Nick**   I don't know if I buy that, Jo.

**Jo**   You know it's the pupils I worry about. I don't know what game Boyd is playing but I don't trust it. I can't help you with this, Nick. Whatever you've got going on with Boyd. I don't want any part of it. I've got to be here for kids.

**Nick**   You were right about what you said about risks. Sometimes safe isn't an option.

**Jo**   What do you mean?

**Nick**   If I tell people then I'll end up in all sorts of trouble and the school will get closed down. But if I don't and the bomb goes off . . . then that's all my fault too because I didn't warn anybody. I'm that fucking cat in the middle of the road and cars are flying passed me and I can't stand still.

*The bell goes.*

**Jo**   Hey, if you're not around at break I'll presume you've been all chopped up and put in the pies at lunch.

**Nick**   Yeah or stuffed into the fucking walls. Who do you reckon's doing the maths club? It's not on the rota.

**Jo**   Nightingale's maths club? I seem to be doing everything else for you today, do you want me to cover it?

**Nick**   No. It's fine. I want to do it.


**Four**

*Later that morning.*

*The basement.*

**Nick** *is sat behind piles and piles of registers.*

**Mr Boyd** *enters.*

**Mr Boyd**   Knock knock.

**Nick**   Mr Boyd.

**Mr Boyd**   Look alive.

**Nick**   Yes, trying to.

**Mr Boyd**   Chilly down here. You could chill in this.

**Nick**   I wondered if I could have a heater down here? There's one in the History storeroom. I wouldn't want to catch a cold.

**Mr Boyd**   Oh you can't catch a cold indoors.

**Nick**   Can't you? I don't know if that's true.

**Mr Boyd**   How are you doing down here, Nick?

**Nick**   I'm making my way through it all. You get into quite a rhythm. Date, sticker, folder, box. It's very straightforward.

**Mr Boyd**   Sorry to give you such an uninspiring task. Someone every year draws the short straw for archiving the registers.

**Nick**   I didn't realise there were straws to be drawn.

**Mr Boyd**   An important and vital . . . a vitally important task. Now I don't want to disturb you any longer, I just wanted to make sure you're still compos mentis. No windows down here and that can send you a little loopy.

**Nick**   Well, if I could have that heater that I mentioned?

**Mr Boyd**   I definitely promise to look into it.

**Nick**   Thank you, Mr Boyd.

**Mr Boyd** *goes to leave.*

**Nick**   Mr Boyd, can I ask you a question?

**Mr Boyd**   Of course.

**Nick**   Now this might sound a little, uh, silly. But you don't have me down here because you're worried I'm going tell people about the bomb . . . Do you?

**Mr Boyd**   Is that what you think, Nick?

**Nick**   Well it just seems a bit of a coincidence to have me down here the day after I find out that there's a bomb under the school.

**Mr Boyd**   Rest assured. You being down here has nothing to do with yesterday.

**Nick**   Well that's a relief.

**Mr Boyd**   But when you say it like that it does sound a bit odd, doesn't it?

**Nick**   What?

**Mr Boyd**   No. Odd is the wrong word. In fact, it doesn't sound odd at all. As a matter of fact it sounds perfectly logical to, in my position, keep you away from the students. If that was my intention. Odd would be to accidentally leak to you some very sensitive information and then let you loose up there telling God knows who.

**Nick**   So . . . I'm confused. Mr Boyd, are you keeping me down here because of the bomb or not?

**Mr Boyd**   Life is quite confusing, isn't it, Nick?

**Nick**   Increasingly so, Mr Boyd.

**Mr Boyd**   Send up a call whenever you like and Mrs Jennings can make you a cup of tea.

**Nick**   Mr Boyd, I had another question.

**Mr Boyd**   Another one? Full of questions today, Nick.

**Nick**   It won't take long. I promise. It's just I had this textbook with me, for what we were going to work on in class today. You see, my Year 11s are doing World War Two at the moment.

**Mr Boyd**   Right.

**Nick**   And this book . . . It happens to be about the Battle of Britain. And, and the Blitz. And I've been reading it this morning . . .

*Beat.*

Mr Boyd, this part of town was never bombed in the Blitz, was it?

**Mr Boyd**   History was never my strong suit. I was a geography man myself.

**Nick**   It says it in here. They can be quite accurate about it. Because they recorded every single strike.

**Mr Boyd**   Yes.

**Nick**   So if the Germans never bombed this area, Mr Boyd, whose bomb is it under our school field?

*Beat.*

I was also reading a bit further on about how, after the war, instead of dismantling all of our own excess weapons and bombs, we, in times, buried them.

**Mr Boyd**   Did you really have time for all this reading this morning, Nick? These registers won't do themselves!

**Nick**   Mr Boyd, before the school expanded, was the Brink owned by the government?

**Mr Boyd**   Well, you'd have to ask the council about that.

**Nick**   Should I ask the council about that?

**Mr Boyd**   No. No, don't do that. Christ. You really do like to pick at scabs, don't you? Pick, pick, pick. They should have called you *Picholas* not . . . not Nicholas. Shouldn't they? Hey?

**Nick**   Are you ok, Mr Boyd?

**Mr Boyd**    They really should have windows in here too. Gets hard to breathe without daylight, doesn't it?

**Nick**    We're underground. I suppose windows would be hard to put in. Can I get you some water?

**Mr Boyd**    I don't want any water, Nick.

*Beat.*

It's true. It's all true. The bomb. The Blitz. The government. Whatever.

**Nick**    There's going to be more than one bomb down there isn't there?

**Mr Boyd**    I imagine so, yes.

**Nick**    We were developing some pretty incredible weapons in that war, Mr Boyd. Some pretty nasty stuff. Who knows what's down there.

**Mr Boyd**    Well you seem to have some pretty colourful ideas, Nick.

**Nick**    Has anyone ever checked the, the . . . what could be coming up out of the ground? Like, radiating out from these bombs?

**Mr Boyd**    What on earth are you talking about?

**Nick**    I worry about whether it could be having an effect on the students. There's a lot of violence at the school. The look in some of their eyes . . . What's growing underneath them? If the public knew about this . . . Mr Boyd, are you wanting to get the school shut down? Is this all a plan to, to get a good position in an academy?

**Mr Boyd**    Is that what you think? Is that what you think this is all about?

**Nick**    I don't know.

**Mr Boyd**    That shines me in a terrible light, Nick.

**Nick**    I know. I'm sorry. I didn't mean it. But we have to do something, right? The school should. The, the council. The government should! Do we need to call the government?

**Mr Boyd**    Nick, you are touching on something far greater than yourself. Greater than any of us here. I must warn you, you are meddling. And I don't think a meddling history teacher would curry much favour with . . . with . . .

**Nick**    With who?

**Mr Boyd**    Forces, Nick. Forces so strong they could crush you into liquid.

*Beat.*

This is a story whereby the likes of us aren't even characters.

**Nick**    So what do we do?

**Mr Boyd**    What do we *do*? For Christ's sake, we do nothing. *Nothing.* We keep our mouths shut and our eyes closed.

**Nick**    I wonder if whatever is under us is causing my dreams. I wonder if it's even caused Mrs Nightingale's cancer. I don't know if I can do nothing, Mr Boyd.

**Mr Boyd**    Ok, Nick. Follow that thought through. What exactly do you intend to do? Really? I mean, I admire this new energy in you but really, what on earth can *you* do? You can't even finish the fucking registers.

*Pause.*

Would you like to join me for lunch?

**Nick**    Lunch? No. No, I . . . Thank you but I have plans. I have to be at . . . I'm going for a walk.

**Mr Boyd** *goes to leave.*

**Mr Boyd**    Nick, you have been exposed to more here than you could have ever imagined. Who knows what damage this information may have caused you. I must warn you. This may manifest itself into a headache.

**Five**

*That lunchtime.*

*Mrs Nightingale's class.*

**Nick**   And so the, the fraction needs to be converted, right? It asks for the answer as a decimal.

**Jessica**   Oh yeah.

**Nick**   So do you remember how we do that?

**Jessica**   I divide it?

**Nick**   Yeah that's right. You divide the top number from the bottom. Do you remember what we call them?

**Jessica**   No.

**Nick**   No, that's fine. They're called the, the . . . Hey you know what, it doesn't matter what they're called, you just need to know how to do it.

**Jessica**   Are you ok, sir?

**Nick**   Yeah. If you just convert the answers to the rest then let me know.

*Pause.*

**Jessica**   Why are the blinds closed, sir?

**Nick**   What? Oh . . . To, to keep the light out. If it's too bright you can't see.

*Beat.*

**Jessica**   You seem a bit distracted today, sir.

**Nick**   What?

**Jessica**   Nothing. Sorry. I'll . . .

**Nick**   No, it's ok to talk. This isn't like normal class. I just didn't hear what you said.

**Jessica**   I said that you seem a little distracted, sir.

**Nick**    Oh. Yeah. No, I'm fine.

**Jessica**    I don't mean it rudely, sir.

**Nick**    No. No, you know what, I haven't been sleeping very well. That's all.

*Pause.*

**Jessica**    Is that why you haven't been in school all day, sir?

**Nick**    I . . . I've been in school. I've just been archiving registers. You noticed I wasn't around?

**Jessica**    We were just told you were going to cover our English class.

**Nick**    Oh. Right. Yeah. No. No, not today. Change of plan.

*Silence.*

What would you do, Jessica, if, say, a friend told you something that, that was meant to be a secret. But you know other people deserve to know about it?

**Jessica**    What kind of secret, sir?

**Nick**    It doesn't really matter about the, the secret exactly. More the point. I mean, it's a secret for a reason. And they think they're protecting people by not . . . not saying.

**Jessica**    Why did they tell me what the secret was if people aren't meant to know?

**Nick**    Because maybe you had a hunch about it. Maybe you kind of already knew.

**Jessica**    A secret about this friend?

**Nick**    No, it's a secret about the world. That this friend knows.

**Jessica**    If I went to the friend about a hunch I had about a secret then maybe it's because I trusted this friend to know what to do about it.

**Nick**   But what if you don't trust your friend's judgement?

**Jessica**   Then why are we friends?

**Nick**   Ok maybe you're not friends. You just know each other. Look, I don't mean to . . . This is getting more complicated than I intended. I, uh . . . It doesn't matter.

*Pause.*

**Jessica**   What are the consequences of the secret? Will people get in trouble?

**Nick**   Yeah. You could say that. People would get hurt.

**Jessica**   Hurt?

**Nick**   Possibly. Maybe. I don't know. There's the potential for it to hurt people.

**Jessica**   Then you have to ignore your friend and tell someone.

**Nick**   You think?

**Jessica**   I mean, that's what I'd do.

**Nick**   Ok, so what if another friend though also said to you that telling people would /

/ *The bell goes.*

Oh hey look. The time. Already. Sorry, look let's crack on with these next time. But you get the rule, yeah?

**Jessica**   Yeah.

**Nick**   That's all it is. You just find the rule and stick to it.

*She goes to leave.*

I don't mean to put pressure on you with . . . I don't mean to burden you with stuff you don't need to worry about.

**Jessica**   I'm not a kid.

**Nick**    No, quite right. But this, it's not what we're meant to be talking about now. This is maths club, not, you know, Nick's anxiety club.

**Jessica**    We want our teachers to tell us the truth.

**Nick**    I don't know if I'm allowed to do that.

**Jessica**    But if you won't tell us the truth, then who will?

**Six**

*That afternoon.*

*The corridor.*

**Jo** *is with* **Nick**.

**Jo**    What are we doing, Nick? Everyone's gone home. I need to get off myself.

**Nick**    This won't take long.

**Jo**    But why are we stood in the corridor outside Boyd's /

**Mr Boyd** *enters*.

**Nick**    Mr Boyd.

**Mr Boyd**    Nick. Jo. How can I help you?

**Nick**    Mr Boyd. Can we have a quick word?

**Jo**    Nick?

**Mr Boyd**    In my office? I've already locked up.

**Nick**    Ok well out here will do.

**Jo**    Nick, what are you doing?

**Nick**    Mr Boyd, the recent revelations about the school have shocked me and, and haunted me. I think we need to tell people the truth about what's underneath the school fields. Because if we won't tell the truth then who will? We're teachers, for Christ's sake. It's what the students, it's what the public, deserve. And, and I know what you're going to say and yes it is very ominous and terrifying and I'm sure there will be consequences with the crushing and the liquid and what-have-you. But, I tell you this, whatever's going on, you can silence one teacher without a hassle but you can't silence two. Jo knows about the bombs. And we won't stand for anything less than a full inquiry and, and an assurance that whatever's under the ground here will be cleared.

*Beat.*

**Mr Boyd**   Is this true, Jo? Are you with Nick in this?

**Jo**   No.

**Nick**   What?

**Jo**   No. I don't know what he's talking about, Mr Boyd.

**Nick**   Jo.

**Jo**   I told you I don't want to be part of this, Nick. You didn't listen to me.

**Nick**   But this is serious. You do know what I'm talking about. Tell him that you do.

**Jo**   I don't want the school to close down.

**Nick**   Jo. I thought you were my friend. I thought you had my back.

**Jo**   I'm here for the kids. Someone has to be. And some rumour about a /

**Nick**   / Rumour? You still don't believe me?

**Jo**   No. I don't believe that there's a bomb under the school.

**Nick**   But, Jo, the Germans didn't even bomb the . . . So you need proof? Is that what this is?

**Mr Boyd**   Look, I'm sorry to have dragged you into this here, Jo. Had I have known . . . I don't mean to be wasting your time.

**Nick**   I can't believe it. You, you're making me out to look insane.

**Jo**   Is there anything else, Mr Boyd?

**Mr Boyd**   No. I'll see you tomorrow.

**Jo** *goes to leave.*

**Nick**   Jo . . . Jo. *Please?*

**Mr Boyd**   Actually, Jo, yes I would like you to hear this.

*She stops.*

Nick, now I want you to know that I respect you deeply. But this whole sorry affair seems to have got us all a little tangled. I wonder whether the best thing here should be that you have a bit of time off. Yes? A bit of time away from the school to cool down.

**Nick**   No . . .

**Mr Boyd**   You need to relax. Maybe go on a holiday.

**Nick**   I don't want to go on a holiday.

**Mr Boyd**   Everybody wants a holiday.

**Nick**   You can't force me out of the school, Mr Boyd.

**Mr Boyd**   But, Nick, you are not well. You're stressed. Ms Fletcher here can attest to that.

**Nick**   I'm not stressed. You said I wasn't stressed. You said I was modern. My phone. Buzzing. Humming fridges. Remember? In our meeting? Mr Boyd, you can't get away with this. You're, you're not only silencing a teacher, you're *excluding* me.

**Jo**   Nick. Maybe we should /

**Nick**   You were there, Mr Boyd. You remember. You were in that room telling me that /

**Mr Boyd**   / What I remember is that yesterday you came to me complaining about some terrible dreams you were having. And I could see how this anxiety was manifesting itself in your behaviour so I decided to, today, give you a solitary and calming task with the registers. It didn't feel right to have you in a classroom. Then I hear at lunchtime you snuck into an extra maths tutorial despite my clear and well-reasoned desire to keep you away from teaching.

**Nick**   But, but if I didn't do it then Jessica wouldn't have /

**Mr Boyd**   / And now this. You've clearly upset Ms Fletcher and you've been, I must say, a little short with me too. So what choice have you left me other than to ask you, politely but firmly, to take a few weeks off?

**Nick**   Jo.

**Jo**   Maybe he's right, Nick. You have been having these dreams. Some time off might do you good.

*Beat.*

**Mr Boyd**   Now I do believe Duncan is working the gates this evening but I wouldn't want to call him to help us end our meeting. Would I?

**Nick**   No. It's fine. I'll go. I'm going.

**Jo**   I'll come with you.

**Nick**   No. I'll go on my own.

*He exits.*

**Mr Boyd**   Goodnight, Nick. Try and get some sleep, poor fellow.


**Seven**

*That night.*

**Martin***'s house.*

**Martin**   And so I can't let that go, can I?

**Chloe**   No you can't, Martin.

**Martin**   And lose face like that? I'd never live it down. You know what I'm saying, don't you, Nick?

**Nick**   Yeah.

**Martin**   Yeah you know it. And so I'm stood there and I'm thinking, come on, you old dog. Show them. Fuck them. You've got to, yeah?

**Nick**   Yeah.

**Martin**   And so I do it. I get on the bike and I just . . .

**Chloe**   Just . . .?

**Martin**   And well I just stack it. Course I do. Completely. I don't know what I'm doing. End up toppling over, right off the bloody slope and I cut my arms all down here and here. In hospital for a week.

**Chloe**   Oh amazing. How funny, Nick.

**Nick**   Yeah. Hilarious.

**Martin**   Thing is though, I showed nerve. And that's what's important. I showed balls. And in life, it's how you act, not how you talk. How are you finding the venison, mate?

**Nick**   Yeah. Yeah, it's lovely.

**Martin**   It's what?

**Nick**   It's lovely, Martin. Really nice.

**Martin**   What I did was I cooked it in a water bath for about two hours and then finished it off in the pan.

**Nick**   Right.

**Chloe**   We were looking at water baths, weren't we?

**Nick**   Were we?

**Chloe**   Yes. Thanks for paying attention.

**Martin** *and* **Chloe** *laugh.*

**Nick**    I thought all baths were water baths.

**Martin**    You won't look back, guys. I can promise you that.

**Chloe**    Don't be silly, Nick.

**Nick**    I'm not.

**Martin**    Do you slow-cook very much, Nick?

**Nick**    Not really.

**Martin**    Well you will do.

**Chloe**    Sold. Let's do it.

**Nick**    I'm not that much of a cook.

**Martin**    What's that, mate?

**Nick**    I said I'm not that much of a cook. Don't know what I'd make of a water bath to be honest.

**Martin**    I don't . . .

**Chloe**    Well, we can learn. Can't we, Nick? We can learn how to use a water bath.

**Nick**    We've barely learnt how to use the hob. We're not that into fancy food, Martin. Normally if it's beige and comes in plastic then we'll just have that and what we don't have for dinner we'd have for breakfast. That's how it works round ours. Can I do a pizza in a water bath?

**Martin**    Well, no.

**Chloe**    You're being silly, Nick.

**Nick**    I'm just being honest.

**Martin**    Nick's hitting on a good point actually. There's nothing wrong with being honest about one's shortcomings.

**Nick**    Shortcomings?

**Chloe**   You know, you're right, Martin. We have to admit that we just don't make enough time for the important things.

**Nick**   Water baths aren't important.

**Martin**   What's that, mate?

**Nick**   I said we're busy people, Martin. You know how it is.

**Martin**   Of course. And how are things going at school, Nick?

**Nick**   Okay. Yeah. Busy.

**Martin**   You getting your homework in on time?

**Nick**   Yeah, yeah. Good one.

**Chloe**   Things are getting better now, aren't they, Nick?

**Nick**   Better? What do you mean?

**Martin**   Chloe told me you've been having some problems.

**Nick**   She did?

**Martin**   Depression, Nick. The black dog.

**Nick**   I'm not depressed.

**Martin**   And nightmares too. Nasty.

**Nick**   Chloe?

**Chloe**   I thought it would help. It was before you said not to. But it's good news now, isn't it? Things are getting better.

**Martin**   And so I thought, what with Nick getting back in the swing of things and us getting ever so closer to a certain someone's birthday . . . Why don't we throw a bit of a party?

**Chloe**   A birthday party? You can't!

**Martin**   Course I don't want to tread on anyone's toes. You hadn't started making plans, had you, Nick?

**Nick**    Started making . . . No, not firm plans no. Ideas, mainly. Keeping it open.

**Martin**    You weren't thinking of taking her out the country, were you?

**Nick**    No.

**Martin**    A weekend away?

**Nick**    No.

**Martin**    A few nights in Paris?

**Nick**    No. I'm . . . Not this year. No.

**Chloe**    We're not really birthday people, Martin.

**Martin**    Everyone's a birthday person, Chloe. What is this, *Angela's Ashes*? You've got to have a birthday party. I was thinking maybe the Grayson.

**Chloe**    The Grayson Hotel? We've always said about a night there, haven't we, Nick?

**Nick**    Yeah.

**Martin**    I thought we could get a band, invite some friends, bring in caterers. Get a fucking planner if we want one.

**Chloe**    We can't get a planner!

**Martin**    Well here I also thought you might want to do it yourself. I know you're like. You'd probably do it better than any of the professionals anyway.

**Chloe**    You know I would enjoy that. I do like to plan, don't I, Nick?

**Martin**    You're a creative spirit. You'd want to be involved. That's why I didn't want it to be a surprise. I hope you don't mind me springing it on you like this, Nick?

**Nick**    What? No. It's just . . .

**Martin**    Just what, mate?

**Chloe**　Just what, Nick?

**Nick**　I mean . . . Oh come on, Chloe, as nice as all this sounds, we can't afford that. It's just not the kind of thing we can do. Is it?

**Chloe**　No, I suppose not.

**Martin**　Nick, you don't understand what I'm saying. I want to do it. As my present to Chloe, to say thank you. And as a gesture to you, mate, after everything you've been through.

**Nick**　You can't do that.

**Martin**　I want to. And want, in this world, is the strongest element known to man. I've never wanted something that I haven't had, Nick.

**Chloe**　Martin, maybe Nick's right. It's too much.

**Martin**　Nothing's too much. Not for us. We've all got decisions to make, Chloe. Every moment, every second, is a crossroads. Do we turn left into obsolescence or do we turn right, to success?

**Chloe**　We turn right, Martin.

**Nick** *laughs.*

**Martin**　Something the matter, mate?

**Chloe**　What are you sniggering at?

**Nick**　Nothing.

**Martin**　Which way do you turn, Nick?

**Nick**　What's that?

**Martin**　At the crossroads. Which way do you turn?

**Nick**　I think I'm pulling over and asking for directions myself, Martin.

**Chloe**　Nick.

**Martin**    I wonder if I could be so bold as to offer you a bit of advice, mate?

**Nick**    Please do.

**Martin**    Honestly, I've got deep respect for you. Really have. It's good to be resilient. And you're doing great. Don't get me wrong. Teaching, man, someone's got to do it. I just think that the defences you have, the mechanisms you use, can sometimes stifle your ambition. You have to be careful that a cycle of stasis doesn't warp how you see the world, see what people are actually doing for you.

**Nick**    Stasis. That's your word.

**Chloe**    It's not my word.

**Martin**    You're not a lazy person, Nick. I know you're not. And I know how easy it is to get stuck. We've all been there. I see you, mate. I see you.

**Nick**    You see me?

**Martin**    I do. It's all about hunger. How hungry are you?

**Nick**    Not very.

**Martin**    No?

**Nick**    Not after two courses of your lovely cooking, no.

**Martin**    Ah! Funny!

**Nick**    No. I really take that to heart, Martin. Particularly coming from you. If you can see it then it must be bloody obvious.

**Chloe**    Nick. Don't be like that.

**Nick**    How should I be, Chloe?

**Martin**    Now, pal.

**Nick**    Pal? Who says pal?

**Martin**    I think I've said something wrong.

**Chloe**   No you haven't. Nick's just being . . .

**Nick**   What am I being, pal?

**Chloe**   Don't pal me.

**Nick**   He pals me.

**Martin**   Friends . . . Let's not lose the table.

**Nick**   Lose the . . . Jesus, you really are a prick.

**Chloe**   Oh my God.

**Nick**   I mean you must sense it, with the shit that comes out of your mouth. I don't expect anyone who works for you to tell you but you must at least hear yourself, no?

**Martin**   I hear myself, Nick. And trust me, no one takes on my advice more than me. And look at where I've got to. So it can't all be that shit, can it?

**Nick**   No. You know what, you're probably right. But there is one thing. You can't have a cycle of stasis. If it's in a cycle then it's not fucking static, is it?

*Beat.*

**Chloe**   Have you finished?

**Nick**   Yes. You know what, yes I have.

## Part Three

### One

*The present. Night time.*

**Nick**   I see this boy there amongst the History block. He's lying in the rubble and, and so I rush over and I pull . . . I pull him up by the, the arm but as I do I hear a kind of rip . . . and as I pull . . . his body tears in half. And I realise he's nothing but parts. Wet, hot parts. So I put him down, I try to, gently. I feel sick but I feel sad too because he's still crying out to me and I just end up standing there . . . Useless. And then at that moment a brilliant light pops and blinds me and I realise it must be a second explosion. I'm flung into the air and I separate into a million bits. That's when I wake up. That's when I always wake up. When I'm in a million bits. And the thing is, I make this happen. I make the whole thing happen again and again because it only happens if I dream it. It only happens if I see it. So it's my fault.

### Two

*Earlier.*

*The morning.*

*In the car.*

**Chloe**   Don't you care?

**Nick**   Of course I care.

**Chloe**   You completely showed yourself up.

**Nick**   I don't think I said anything unreasonable.

**Chloe**   You were rude to him the whole night.

**Nick**   Come on. He was being a dick.

**Chloe**   No. The only dick there was you. I can't believe it. I had to sit there listening to you do that to my boss. Do you have any idea how that made me feel?

**Nick**   He was taking the piss out of me and you know he was. That should bother you. That's the kind of behaviour you should be pissed off with.

**Chloe**   You're frustrated with your own life so you're lashing out.

**Nick**   Lashing out? I was telling the truth.

**Chloe**   You know what the scary thing is? I really think you believe that. I should've seen this coming. We've been in a rut for so long you're scared.

**Nick**   Scared of what?

**Chloe**   Everything, Nick. You're scared of everything, you're petrified of change. It's the school that's done this.

**Nick**   You don't know what you're talking about. It's the likes of Martin, who just plough through life doing fuck-all for anyone else and yet spout such drivel about /

**Chloe**   / Nick.

**Nick**   About taking opportunities and crossroads and/

**Chloe**   / Nick. I'm not talking about Martin anymore.

**Nick**   There's no point pretending, Chloe. All that kind of thing. It just isn't us.

**Chloe**   No, Nick. I think it just isn't you.

*Beat.*

Whatever you've got going on, you need to work it out. Now. I can't stand by and wait anymore. You know that, don't you?

**Nick**   Pull in here.

**Chloe**   Where?

**Nick**    Here. I'm going to walk through the park today.

**Chloe**    But it's almost nine.

**Nick**    I know what I'm doing, Chloe.

**Three**

*That lunchtime.*

*Mrs Nightingale's class.*

**Jessica** *is sat at a desk.*

**Nick** *enters.*

**Nick**    Hey, sorry I'm late.

**Jessica**    Sir?

**Jo** *appears.*

**Jo**    Nick. What are you doing here?

**Nick**    What am *I* doing here? What, what are *you* doing here? This is my maths club.

**Jo**    You're not meant to be here, Nick.

**Nick**    Hello, Jessica. What are we working on today?

**Jessica**    Still the fractions, sir.

**Jo**    You have to leave, Nick.

**Nick**    Jo, look, I understand. I really do. I wanted to talk to you and I wanted to explain. I completely really understand why you did what you did and maybe I would have done the same thing too in your position. But the thing is I also think you'd do what I'm doing as well. And the problem is you can't see what I can see and I don't think you really appreciate what's going on here.

**Jo**    We have to talk about this another time, Nick. Not in front of a student.

**Jessica**    Should I leave, Ms?

**Jo**    Yes.

**Nick**    No . . . Jessica, no. We can't keep sheltering these students from what's important.

**Jo**    I can't lose my job by being associated with you in this.

**Nick**    That's all you care about, Jo? Your job?

**Jo**    This is serious shit to me. And if I get sacked because I'm too close to you, or if the school shuts because of your crazy rumour then I'm going to be on my arse. I'm not going to get a job in the academies. I've spent my entire career protesting against them.

**Nick**    You told Boyd about me doing the maths club yesterday. You ratted me out so it wouldn't look like we're friends.

**Jo**    Nick, I care about you but I can't let you destroy other people's lives for this. You shouldn't be in the building. If you go now then I won't tell Boyd. I don't even know why you'd risk it. I don't even know why you're here.

**Nick**    I'm here to ask for help.

**Jo**    Well I've told you. I can't help you in the way you need.

**Nick**    I don't mean help from you.

**Jessica** *stands.*

**Jessica**    I believe in you, sir.

**Jo**    Jessica.

**Jessica**    I believe in you, sir! The truth! We need the truth!

**Jo**    Jessica, get out. Now.

**Jessica**    No.

**Jo**    Jessica Havens, I will have you suspended.

**Jessica** *leaves.*

**Jo**   Are you determined to rip this place apart? Whose help were you after, Nick? Don't tell me you've told any of the students.

**Nick**   I've got to stop this, Jo. That's what my dreams mean. It's up to me. It always has been. The bombs are going. And then once they've gone, once there are no bombs, then there won't be any more dreams either. Don't you see? Getting rid of the bombs will stop everything.

**Jo**   If you don't leave now I will call the police. Nick, this is it. This has to be it.

### Four

*That evening?*

*At home.*

**Nick**   Chloe? Hello? Chloe, it's me. Look, I suppose we should chat.

**Martin** *enters.*

**Martin**   Nick.

**Nick**   Martin?

**Martin**   Sorry, mate, I didn't realise you were coming over. I've only put enough in for two.

**Nick**   Put enough in of what? Why are you here?

**Martin**   I suppose I could quickly chuck in another bit. The water bath's only just kicking up.

**Nick**   Water bath? What are you talking about? What are you doing here?

**Martin**   How was school?

**Nick**   Fine. But I don't /

**Martin**   / Any homework?

**Nick**   Martin, is Chloe home?

**Martin**   I'm sure she'll be down in a minute.

**Nick**   Down?

**Martin**   Are you ok, mate? You're looking tired.

**Nick**   I didn't expect to see you here.

**Martin**   What did you expect?

**Nick**   What?

**Martin**   What did you expect? Really?

**Nick**   I expected to talk to Chloe. We've got a lot of things to talk about.

**Martin**   You're a good man, Nick. You're one of life's good guys.

**Nick**   Why do you say that?

**Martin**   Because it's true. And it's sad because you know more than anyone that being good doesn't mean that you win.

**Nick**   Win what? What are you talking about? Where's Chloe? Chloe?

**Chloe** *enters.*

**Chloe**   Nick.

**Nick**   What's going on? Why's Martin here?

**Chloe**   What do you mean *why's Martin here*, why the hell are you here?

**Nick**   What?

**Chloe**   You can't just expect to waltz back in here, Nick. You get out of the car one morning and I don't see you for a week.

**Nick**   A what? A week?

**Chloe**    The fuck were you playing at?

**Martin**    You do smell a bit, mate. Smells like the park.

**Nick**    What are you talking about? I've been out for a day.

**Chloe**    I was worried sick.

**Nick**    I went to the school and then I walked right back. It's the same fucking day, Chloe.

**Martin**    Now don't get angry, pal.

**Nick**    And this. What the fuck is this about? I mean I say a day and you say a week but it's still a bit fucking quick to start an affair.

**Martin**    Start?

**Chloe**    Nick, it's only an affair if there was still love in the relationship.

**Nick**    That's not the dictionary definition, Chloe. Where's all my stuff?

**Chloe**    Your van collected it.

**Nick**    What?

**Chloe**    We put your stuff out. A van collected it right away. We thought that was you.

**Nick**    When have I ever mentioned to you about owning a fucking van, Chloe?

**Martin**    Are you succumbing to dark thoughts, Nick?

**Nick**    What?

**Martin**    Do you feel as though you are being crushed to liquid?

**Nick**    What? Where did you /

**Chloe**    / Jo rang three days ago asking about you. You didn't tell me you'd been suspended.

**Nick**    I'm not suspended. I'm on holiday.

**Martin**    Nice holiday.

**Nick**    What?

**Chloe**    Have you spoken to her?

**Martin**    To a dark liquid, mate. I see you. I see you.

**Nick**    Chloe, Martin's really pissing me off.

**Chloe**    Can you go and get Nick a glass of water please, Martin?

**Martin**    Course.

*He exits.*

**Nick**    Why he's getting me water from my own fucking kitchen. That's my water, Chloe. He doesn't even know where the glasses are.

**Chloe**    He knows where the glasses are, Nick. I don't want you getting angry.

**Nick**    I'm not angry.

**Chloe**    We all just need to keep calm.

**Nick**    I am calm. I'm fucking calm, Chloe.

**Chloe**    We were just at a crossroads . . . And you went one way and I went . . . the other.

**Nick**    Chloe, if you knew, if you had any idea about the things that are going on right now . . . Everything's changed. The bombs have changed everything.

**Chloe**    What bombs? What are you talking about?

**Nick**    I never wanted this. I never wanted any of it. I just want everything to go back to the way it was.

**Chloe**    But the way it was doesn't exist anymore. And that's a good thing. Isn't it?

**Martin** *comes back with a glass of water.*

**Chloe**   Why don't you have some water, Nick?

**Nick**   I don't want any fucking water.

**Martin**   Hey, don't get aggressive about the water, mate.

**Nick**   It's not the water, Martin. It's the fucker holding it.

**Martin**   Look I think it's time we called it a night, hey?

**Nick**   Yes, I think that's a good idea. Thanks, Martin.

*Beat.*

Oh what, you mean for *me* to call it a night? For me to go?

**Martin**   I think it's for the best, pal. Don't you?

**Nick**   Chloe?

**Chloe**   Think of this as an opportunity, Nick. To start again.

**Nick**   Chloe, I really need you to understand because I'm about to do something incredible. The bombs, Chloe. I'm going to get rid of the bombs.

**Martin**   It's nice to have a project.

**Chloe**   Nick, you have so much potential. It's what I fell in love with in the first place. Some day you're going to find yourself again. We're all going to be proud of you.

**Nick**   The bombs.

**Chloe**   So proud.


**Five**

*That night. The present.*

*The moment after* **Nick** *has finished his monologues.*

*The Brink.*

**Nick**   And so that's it. That's the dream. And every night I go through the same pattern, stuck in this cycle where I'm helpless. But I'm not helpless in real life. Am I?

**Jessica** *appears. We realise it is her he has been talking to in the present.*

**Jessica**   I don't think so, sir.

**Nick**   But I can't help thinking that if I hadn't have had the dreams then maybe they wouldn't exist. If I hadn't have known about it then maybe it would never explode.

**Jessica**   But it still would've been down there. Except no one would have known except Boyd.

**Nick**   Boyd and, and the government. Remember the government.

**Jessica**   Yes. So you needed to have the dreams, you needed the dreams to save us, sir.

**Nick**   Yes. Yes, you're right. But please call me Nick.

**Jessica**   Nick. I had to lie to my mum tonight. She asked where I was going and I didn't know what to say. What *are* we doing out here, sir . . . I mean, Nick.

**Nick**   Don't you see? This is it. And, and you told me to tell the truth. Well this is the truth. And we're going to end it. Me and you.

**Jessica**   How? Are you going to get Mr Boyd arrested?

**Nick**   What? No.

**Jessica**   Then what are you going to do?

**Nick**   Underneath us here, Jessica, are the bombs. My dreams, all of this, has been leading me to here. And I'm going to dig them up.

*He picks up a spade and starts digging.*

*Bright spotlights. The sound of a helicopter. The sound of trucks.*

**Jessica** *runs away.*

**Mr Boyd** (*in a megaphone, off*)    Get away! Get out of the way!

**Nick**    Stop! Wait! I'm a teacher!

**Mr Boyd** (*in a megaphone, off*)    Out of the way!

**Nick**    Mr Boyd? You're blinding me.

**Mr Boyd** *enters.*

**Mr Boyd**    Nick, what the hell are you doing?

**Nick**    Mr Boyd, am I dying?

**Mr Boyd**    Of course you're not. You shouldn't be here.

**Nick**    What's going on?

**Mr Boyd**    This isn't safe for you, Nick. You need to leave.

**Nick**    What are all these people doing?

**Mr Boyd**    They're digging up the bombs.

**Nick**    I'm digging up the bombs.

**Mr Boyd**    No, Nick. No, you're not. You weren't here. You saw none of this.

**Nick**    I need to do this.

**Mr Boyd**    Oh mark my words, Nick. You are central to events here. This is all happening because of you. You spooked them, you've worried them. And they've always been troubled, Nick. They're troubled people at the best of times. The *tempers* . . . I wanted to get that across to you. There are going to be repercussions, I've been told to tell you that. I'm sorry.

**Nick**    Look at them, Mr Boyd. Look at how many of them there were. Seeing them out of the ground, I'm already feeling so much better.

**Mr Boyd**    Incredible, isn't it?

**Nick**    What are they going to do with the hole?

**Mr Boyd**    You don't need to know that. You don't need to know anything anymore, Nick.

**Nick**    I've really done it, haven't I, Mr Boyd? I've really messed with the order of things.

**Mr Boyd**    You had the fear of a young man in you. Inspiring, in a way. I'm sorry I didn't protect you.

**Nick**    What should I do now, Mr Boyd? I can't go home.

**Mr Boyd**    Nick, I don't think there's very much you can do. What you seem to have done throughout this whole sorry affair is gradually and systemically limit your choices down to one.

**Nick**    Jessica? Do you mean Jessica?

**Mr Boyd**    I mean your exit.

**Nick**    The park. I could go to the park.

**Mr Boyd**    Nick, wait.

**Nick** *exits.*


**Six**

*The next day. Thursday morning.*

*The park.*

**Nick** *wakes up on the ground. Student* **One** *is stood over him.*

**One**    Sir . . .? Sir . . .? Are you ok, sir?

**Nick**    What's going on?

**One**    You were asleep, sir.

**Nick**    What?

**One**    You were asleep in the park, sir. Shit.

**Nick**   Don't fuss. And don't swear. Help me find my shoe.

*They look.*

Have you ever seen the sun rise over the buildings there? It makes such a beautiful shape. It's like they're designed like that on purpose. For that moment right there. And we're having it now. You and me.

*Beat.*

What do you want?

**One**   Nothing.

**Nick**   What do you mean *nothing*? Got to want something. What are you doing?

**One**   I just saw you lying there, sir. I'm on my way to school.

**Nick**   To school?

**One**   Here's where I meet my girlfriend. Are you ok, sir? Do you need me to get you someone?

**Nick**   What? No. I'm fine. I'm good. I'm great. Waking up for once in a really good mood. Look at the sky. So bright. Come on.

**One**   Come on?

**Nick**   Don't want to be late. I'll walk with you.

**One**   Late for what?

**Nick**   School, you dumbo! Don't want to start your day with a black mark, do you?

**One**   Jess isn't here yet, sir.

**Nick**   What?

**One**   My girlfriend isn't here yet, sir. Here's where I meet her.

**Nick**   What did you say, what's her name?

**One**   Jessica Havens, sir. You know her, sir. She's in your maths club.

**Nick**   Is Jessica really your, your girlfriend?

**One**   Yes, sir.

**Nick**   Surely you're too young.

**One**   We've not done full sex, if that's what you're /

**Nick**   / No, I mean you're too young *for her*. You're just a boy.

**One**   We're in the same class, sir.

**Nick**   She never said.

**One**   Said what?

**Nick**   She never told me she had a boyfriend.

**One**   Why would she, sir?

**Nick**   Why?

**One**   Yeah.

**Nick**   Because we tell each other everything.

**One**   I love her, sir.

**Nick**   No, you don't. Don't be . . . You don't even understand what that means.

**One**   You don't know that, pal.

**Nick**   Hey, don't call me pal.

**One**   You don't think she loves Matthew Timms, do you, sir?

**Nick**   What?

**One**   Matthew Timms, sir. You don't think she loves him, do you, sir? Because he started a rumour that he fingered her behind the bins behind the English block but I couldn't hit him because it was before we were going out and because it wasn't true. Sir.

**Nick**    No she doesn't love Matthew Timms.

**One**    Oh good.

**Nick**    She loves me.

**One**    What?

**Nick**    She doesn't love Matthew Timms and she doesn't love you. She loves me.

**One** *starts to laugh in disbelief.*

**One**    Sir?

**Nick**    Why are you laughing? Stop laughing.

**One**    I'm sorry, Nick.

**Nick**    Don't call me Nick.

**One**    Come on, pal. It was a joke!

**Nick**    I told you to stop calling me pal.

**One**    You're stressed. You've got to sleep, Nick. Sleep's important for a healthy brain.

**Nick**    I see what this is. I see what you are.

**One**    I'm just a student, sir.

**Nick**    You're *them* and you're here to crush me into a liquid. Well, it's too late. You can do what you like but the truth is it's over. The bombs are gone. I stopped it.

**One**    Then why's it still ticking?

**Nick**    What?

**One**    Tick tick tick.

*He laughs uncontrollably.*

**Nick**    Stop laughing, don't laugh at me. Hey, stop it. Shut up. Shut up. Come here.

*He lunges at* **One**. *Grabs him by the collar.*

**One**    This may manifest itself into a headache.

*Blackout.*

*A moment.*

*Lights rise.*

**Jessica** *is stood alone. She is sobbing.*

*We see* **Nick**'s *back. He is hunched into a bush.*

**Jessica**    What have you done? What have you done?

**Nick** *stands. His front is covered head to toe in blood.*

**Nick**    Jessica.

**Jessica**    I can't believe you've done this.

**Nick**    We have to get out of here, Jessica. We have to go right away.

**Jessica**    No.

**Nick**    No? What . . .

**Jessica**    I can't believe you've . . . You've gone too far, sir.

**Nick**    How can you say that? It was . . . That wasn't real, Jessica. That wasn't . . . That was *them*.

**Jessica**    He was my *boyfriend*, Nick.

**Nick**    What? No, he . . . You never told me you had a boyfriend.

**Jessica**    Why would I tell you?

**Nick**    Because we told each other the truth.

**Jessica**    I don't think we can talk anymore. My mum says.

**Nick**    Don't be silly. Why are you being silly?

**Jessica**    I shouldn't have come with you to the Brink last night. She's angry with me, sir.

**Nick**    Hey, come on. Call me Nick.

**Jessica**    I don't want to call you Nick anymore.

**Nick**    Don't say that.

**Jessica**    You're in a lot of trouble, sir. You're in a lot of trouble now.

**Nick**    I don't care.

**Jessica**    But you have to.

**Nick**    Why?

**Jessica**    Because you're an adult. You have to be an adult otherwise we can't be children. And if no one teaches us properly now then how can we ever be grown-ups?

**Nick**    I told you the truth.

**Jessica**    But it meant something different to you, sir.

*Further into the park.*

*The world is disintegrating.*

**Mr Boyd** *is there.*

**Mr Boyd**    Look alive, Nick.

**Nick**    Yes, trying to. They came for me, Mr Boyd. And I didn't take it. I stood up for myself.

**Mr Boyd**    What?

**Nick**    Them. They came for me. Because of the bomb. And . . . and they weren't expecting me to fight back.

**Mr Boyd**    No, Nick. They haven't come for you yet.

**Nick**    But that was . . .

**Mr Boyd**    That was just a student.

**Nick**　Oh.

**Mr Boyd**　There's going to be a lot of paperwork, Nick. A lot of paperwork, indeed.

**Nick**　What happens now?

**Mr Boyd**　Now? Now you've hurt a student, now they come for you.

**Nick**　Did they mean for that to happen, did they . . . Was Jessica . . . Mr Boyd, I'm confused.

**Mr Boyd**　Think of a cup, Nick. And think of pouring water into that cup. And you're pouring and pouring and pouring until the cup is full. And if you don't stop pouring. What happens?

**Nick**　You make a mess.

**Mr Boyd**　You make a mess. And that's what this is. This is a mess.

**Nick**　You know there's one thing I wish I did differently. I wish I listened more to people who didn't think they knew what they were on about. They tell us so much, every day. I wish I listened more to doubt. Can I ask you something?

**Mr Boyd**　Anything, Nick.

**Nick**　Was I a good teacher, Mr Boyd?

**Mr Boyd**　You just might be the very worst teacher I have ever laid my eyes on, Nick.

*A bolt of light flashes across the park.*

*A cacophony of noise (a chorus of angels?) lifts* **Nick** *into the air before he separates into a million pieces.*

**End**

# Black Mountain

## Characters

**Rebecca**
**Paul**
**Helen**

## Set and Sound

*The world is built with light and sound.*

*Everything is off stage. Things such as the grate, the wood shed and the kettle are gestured into the darkness.*

*The only things that can actually exist in the space are the people, the torch and the axe.*

## Note on the Text

*(. . .) denotes speech trailing off*

*(/) and (\) denotes interruption*

*Punctuation is to suggest delivery rather than conform to the rules of grammar*

*Beats < Pauses < Silences*

## Day One

**One**

*Morning.*

*A bedroom in a house in a forest.*

*The sound of birds in the trees.*

**Rebecca** *is looking out of the window.*

*A knock.*

**Rebecca**   Hey.

**Paul**   Sorry. I didn't know if you were up.

**Rebecca**   Yeah. Come in.

**Paul**   I, uh, just wanted to say I've put coffee on. Downstairs.

**Rebecca**   Oh. Great. Thanks. I'll come down now.

*He notices the view from the window.*

**Paul**   Oh wow.

**Rebecca**   Yeah.

**Paul**   I wasn't sure if you'd get any light, with the trees so . . .

**Rebecca**   Yeah.

**Paul**   But it's bright. Really bright in here.

**Rebecca**   It's beautiful. To wake up to. Yeah.

**Paul**   How did you sleep?

*She shakes her head.*

Oh. Sorry.

**Rebecca**   No, it's . . . I mean, it takes me a while to get used to new places anyway.

**Paul**   Yeah.

*Beat.*

**Rebecca**   What room are you in?

**Paul**   I'm across the hall.

**Rebecca**   How is it?

**Paul**   Yeah, it's, it doesn't, the trees don't break so much on that side.

**Rebecca**   Oh, right.

**Paul**   So it's not as light.

**Rebecca**   Yeah.

**Paul**   But it's nice, though. I like it. You know what, the, the, I think I'm feeling it already.

**Rebecca**   That's good.

**Paul**   Yeah.

*Beat.*

Anyway, I'll let you . . .

*He goes to leave.*

**Rebecca**   You were up. Early. You were up early, this morning.

**Paul**   Oh. Was I?

**Rebecca**   I could hear you. Downstairs. Through the grate in the wall, there.

*She gestures to a wall. He notices the grate, which is at ankle height.*

**Paul**   Huh. Look at that.

**Rebecca**   It echoes everything going on in the kitchen.

**Paul**   I, I didn't know.

**Rebecca**    No.

**Paul**    I'm sorry.

**Rebecca**    Don't be sorry. I'm just saying.

**Paul**    If I'd have known I'd have been quieter.

**Rebecca**    No, it's not your fault. I was up. The daylight woke me.

**Paul**    But still. You don't want to, have to, hear me wandering around first thing. Do you want to swap, change rooms or something?

**Rebecca**    No. No it's fine. I was just wondering what you were up to is all.

**Paul**    Oh. Right. Yeah. Well, I mean, nothing.

**Rebecca**    Nothing?

**Paul**    I, I put some coffee on, but, but apart from that, I, I . . .

**Rebecca**    You know I didn't even think to pack things like coffee.

**Paul**    No. Neither did I. Actually, I, I found a tin in the cupboard.

**Rebecca**    Oh.

**Paul**    So I don't know how long it's been there. I should say. Might be crap, I don't know. We'll have to try it.

**Rebecca**    Did you find anything else?

**Paul**    No. Not uh, I mean, there's a few Stephen Kings. So that's handy, if uh, if we end up at each other's throats or something.

**Rebecca**    Yeah.

**Paul**    Hey you know what, what would be a good idea? Uh, going and getting supplies. We should probably go and . . .

**Rebecca**   Yeah.

**Paul**   Get stuff. Stock up.

**Rebecca**   Yeah, good idea.

**Paul**   Because there's nothing. Like, apart from the coffee. There's nothing here. And even that might be . . .

**Rebecca**   We could go this morning.

**Paul**   Yeah. Great.

**Rebecca**   Unless you had something planned?

**Paul**   No, I've not got . . . I've no plans, no. Should I have?

**Rebecca**   No, no.

**Paul**   Ok. Because I was like, then I was like, oh shit, was I meant to, you know, an itinerary or something?

**Rebecca**   Oh. Fuck no. No.

**Paul**   No. Good ok. Well let's, let's go get stuff then. Let's go shop.

**Rebecca**   Yeah.

**Paul**   I don't know where, but.

**Rebecca**   Well did they leave a note?

**Paul**   Uh, did they . . . what?

**Rebecca**   Did they leave a note, about where to go, for, for stuff?

**Paul**   Uh . . . No.

*His eye is drawn to the grate.*

**Rebecca**   They said they were going to leave a note for us.

**Paul**   Right. Did they?

**Rebecca**   With directions and a . . . Because otherwise you could be driving for hours.

**Paul**   No. Yeah. Sure. It makes sense, but uh . . . Well, we've got the sat nav, so . . .

**Rebecca**   So there wasn't a note?

**Paul**   Uh, well not that I . . . No. I didn't see one.

**Rebecca**   Weird.

**Paul**   But, I mean . . . We'll be fine.

**Rebecca**   Yeah, they just said they were going to. With numbers and /

**Paul**   / Numbers? For what?

**Rebecca**   For if something happened.

**Paul**   Right ok. Well, we've got our phones, if uh.

**Rebecca**   Do you even get signal here?

**Paul**   Yeah. Yeah. I mean, I will do.

*Beat.*

You know what. There's the neighbour. We can ask them, if we need to, to . . . call anyone.

**Rebecca**   The neighbour?

**Paul**   Yeah. And they'll know where the village is too.

**Rebecca**   I didn't even, I thought there wasn't anyone in next door.

**Paul**   Yeah. Yeah there's . . . Somebody.

**Rebecca**   Have you been out already?

**Paul**   Oh, no. No, I, I, just saw the curtains. I just saw that the curtains, they're open now. So. They were closed when we got here. And.

**Rebecca**   Right.

**Paul**   So maybe we can ask them. About where to go. Instead of worrying about a note or directions or whatever.

**Rebecca**    Maybe they'll be able to show us how to turn the heating on.

**Paul**    Yeah. Yeah, maybe.

**Rebecca**    That'd be handy.

**Paul**    I mean, there's the fire. If worst comes to worst.

**Rebecca**    A fire?

**Paul**    Yeah. In the, did you see it?

**Rebecca**    Yeah, I just . . . Do we know how to use a fire?

**Paul**    Yeah. I do. I, I had one. When I was a kid.

**Rebecca**    Oh. Did you?

**Paul**    Yeah. They used to uh, my folks had one. They used to put me in charge of it. My dad used to say go feed the uh, as in it ate wood, go feed the eater. Huh. Funny, the things you . . . There's the shed for it. Down there.

*They look out the window.*

See it? Under that tree.

**Rebecca**    Oh yeah.

**Paul**    You see it?

**Rebecca**    I wondered what that was.

**Paul**    It's the wood shed. It's got everything. A wheelbarrow, axe. A torch, which is, uh, good to remember. And you know what, it's stacked to the ceiling with, with wood. So if we need to use it, the, the, it'll outlast us, the pile. I'm sure.

*Beat.*

So I can just /

**Rebecca**    / You've seen it? Inside the shed?

**Paul**    The, uh? Yeah.

**Rebecca**    You've been out to the shed?

**Paul**    Yeah, just a quick, uh.

**Rebecca**    I thought you said you hadn't been outside.

**Paul**    Oh. Did I?

**Rebecca**    Yeah. I asked about the neighbours and you said you hadn't been out.

**Paul**    Oh uh, yeah. But I've, I've been out to the shed. I, uh . . . I had the time. I had the time because I thought you were asleep.


**Two**

*Afternoon.*

*The kitchen of the house.*

*There's a door leading to outside, there's a door leading to the rest of the house.*

**Paul** *and* **Rebecca** *enter from outside.*

**Paul**    Are you ok?

**Rebecca**    Yeah. Just a bit shaken up.

*He tries to give her space.*

*He starts to pace around.*

How about you?

*He hasn't heard.*

Paul?

**Paul**    Oh uh, yeah. Yeah I'm fine. I'm just . . .

**Rebecca**    You're pacing.

**Paul**    I'm what?

**Rebecca**    You're pacing. Pacing about.

**Paul**   Oh. Sorry. Yeah.

**Paul** *stops*.

I mean it's so . . .

**Rebecca**   Yeah.

**Paul**   I mean, he could have killed someone.

**Rebecca**   Yeah.

**Paul**   Driving like that. It's, it's, but not that he cared. You know? That he . . . Hey, did you get his number plate?

**Rebecca**   No.

**Paul**   No. Neither did I. How could you with the, uh, the speed he was going. Big car too. These aren't roads you go fast on. Locals, see. The only people who drive like that on roads like this are the locals. They're a, a law unto themselves. Don't you think?

*Beat.*

Don't you think?

**Rebecca**   Yeah.

**Paul**   Yeah. I do too.

*Beat.*

You know what, I'm going to, to, I'm going to knock on next door and, and . . .

**Rebecca**   Next door?

**Paul**   And I'm going to ask them about the car.

**Rebecca**   Paul.

**Paul**   And, you know what, I'm going to go back to the village and, and ask people there too. There can't be that many cars like that driving about.

**Rebecca**   What do you mean ask about the car?

**Paul**   I'm gonna say, I'm gonna tell them what happened and, and ask them whether they know who it is. Driving about in a car like that.

**Rebecca**   You're not going to do that.

**Paul**   Why not?

**Rebecca**   They're not going to know who it is.

**Paul**   They might do.

**Rebecca**   And even if they do, what are you going to do about it? Knock on his door? And then what? Tell him off? Get in a fight? Then what?

*Beat.*

Then what?

**Paul**   So you don't want me to say anything.

**Rebecca**   I just don't know what you can actually do about it, Paul.

*Beat.*

**Paul**   I'm allowed to be angry. I can be angry. You can't just, he can't just go around disregarding people like that.

**Rebecca**   I know. It just . . .

**Paul**   What?

**Rebecca**   It doesn't matter. Really. Does it?

*Beat.*

**Paul**   You know what, if this was any other time in our lives, then I reckon it would matter. Yeah.

*Pause.*

**Rebecca**   Look, why don't you go and get some rest? Go have a sleep or something?

**Paul**   You think?

**Rebecca**    Yeah, you drove half the night and you were up early this morning. You should go and have a rest.

**Paul**    Yeah, maybe.

**Rebecca**    It might make you feel better.

**Paul**    Yeah, well let's see. I mean, we're having a rest, aren't we? It's all a, a rest, isn't it, so.

**Rebecca**    It's uh, it's what?

**Paul**    Um. I mean, we've got time to, to . . .

**Rebecca**    It's all a rest?

**Paul**    What I meant was that the, the week /

**Rebecca**    / A rest.

**Paul**    Not a rest, as such.

**Rebecca**    Is this a . . . Paul, is this a holiday to you?

*Beat.*

**Paul**    No. I, I . . . I mean, obviously it's not a . . .

**Rebecca**    The point of us being here /

**Paul**    / I know.

**Rebecca**    The only reason that I'd come away with you /

**Paul**    / I know, I do, I /

**Rebecca**    / You said you wanted to, to . . . You asked me. To come.

**Paul**    Rebecca.

**Rebecca**    To talk.

**Paul**    I know.

**Rebecca**    I didn't come on a fucking holiday with you, Paul.

**Paul**    No. I know. I'm sorry. It, it was the wrong word.

*Beat.*

It was the wrong. Yeah.

*Beat.*

I'm going to, hey, I'm gonna get the bags from the, the car.

*He goes to leave.*

**Rebecca**  It can wait. You don't need to . . .

**Paul**  No, it's fine. I'm gonna clear my head and have a smoke anyway.

*He goes to leave again.*

**Rebecca**  You're going to uh. So you're smoking.

**Paul**  Uh. Yeah. I uh.

**Rebecca**  No, I just . . .

**Paul**  Yeah.

**Rebecca**  I didn't think . . .

**Paul**  Didn't think I was smoking?

**Rebecca**  Yeah. I suppose. I don't know.

**Paul**  Do you mind?

**Rebecca**  No, I . . . I just didn't realise you started again. Is all.

**Paul**  No. Well I didn't mean to.

**Rebecca**  Yeah.

**Paul**  Just after everything.

**Rebecca**  No. Sure.

**Paul**  I mean, I don't have to.

**Rebecca**  No. It's fine.

**Paul**  If it's a problem.

**Rebecca**    You know what, you should smoke if you need to.

**Paul**    Well, it's . . . Huh. It's not that I need to, Rebecca.

**Rebecca**    Ok.

**Paul**    And you obviously don't want me to otherwise you wouldn't have said.

**Rebecca**    I was just asking.

**Paul**    It's fine. I won't smoke.

**Rebecca**    Paul, you don't have to say that.

**Paul**    What do you mean *say*?

**Rebecca**    I mean *say* as in say. I don't . . .?

**Paul**    You said *say* like that like I don't have to say I'm not going to smoke because you think I'm going to smoke anyway.

**Rebecca**    That's not what I meant.

**Paul**    Isn't it?

**Rebecca**    No, Paul. Jesus. I said say like that, like *say*, because I don't want you promising something that's too hard to keep.

**Paul**    That's exactly what I'm saying you said.

**Rebecca**    No, because you're saying it with a tone.

**Paul**    A tone?

**Rebecca**    The wrong tone.

**Paul**    It's what it sounded like to me.

**Rebecca**    An edge. There was an edge to it.

**Paul**    An edge. Ok. I don't need to smoke. I don't want to smoke.

**Rebecca**    You don't have to say that.

**Paul**    Maybe I do. For the time we're here I won't smoke. You know it's, it's symbolic. Or whatever.

**Rebecca**    I don't want symbolic.

**Paul**    Well then what the hell do you want?

**Three**

*Night.*

*Outside the wood shed.*

*Dark.*

*The sound of a black bag being dumped in a bin.*

*Beat.*

*A light switches on, triggered by a sensor.*

*It's* **Paul***, walking back to the house.*

*The light flickers. He stops to watch it.*

*The light cuts out. Pitch black.*

**Paul**    Shit.

*The light snaps back on.* **Helen** *is stood in front of* **Paul***. He jumps.*

**Helen**    Paul.

**Paul** *jumps.*

*He recognises her.*

**Paul**    Helen?

*He pulls her away from the view of the house.*

What the, what, what, what /

**Helen**    / Paul, calm down.

**Paul**    Helen, what the hell are you /

**Helen**    / Don't shout. She'll hear you.

**Paul**   What the fuck are you doing?

**Helen**   I'm on holiday. Only joking. Can you imagine?
Your face.

**Paul**   Helen, are you, you *stalking* us?

**Helen**   I'm not stalking you, Paul. Jesus.

**Paul**   Then how did you know we were out here?

**Helen**   You didn't answer your phone.

**Paul**   I told you not to call.

**Helen**   You can't just disappear.

**Paul**   I didn't, I didn't disappear.

**Helen**   You tried to though. You were out here. Before.
The pair of you. But I waited. I waited until you were on
your own. I waited until it was dark.

**Paul**   How long have you been here?

**Helen**   I thought you'd appreciate that.

**Paul**   So you've been . . . This is probably illegal, Helen.

**Helen**   It's not illegal. You were always so overdramatic.

**Paul**   If she, if Rebecca saw you out here then, then she'd
kill us both.

**Helen**   See?

**Paul**   I'm serious.

*Beat.*

What do you want?

**Helen**   I want to talk.

**Paul**   *Talk?* Jesus, Helen. You want to, you've come out all
this way, you're hiding in the fucking bushes, to, to talk? No.
What do you really want?

**Helen**    For some people talking is important. To know how others feel.

**Paul**    Don't give me that.

**Helen**    You ignored me, Paul. You drove me here.

**Paul**    I was, I'm getting on with my life.

**Helen**    Oh, really?

**Paul**    Yeah, I was . . . I was getting on, I was fixing. I was fixing what, what . . .

**Helen**    Fixing. Well good for you.

**Paul**    And, and you can't, you *won't,* you can't start interfering now.

**Helen**    No. No, no, no. You don't deserve to do that to people, Paul. You can't just come in, and then, just, just cut people away.

**Paul**    I didn't, I wasn't, I had to make a choice. In my life. And I'm, I'm sorry that it, it . . . I'm trying to save what, with, what I have with Rebecca.

**Helen**    You are?

**Paul**    Yes.

**Helen**    And how's that going?

*Beat.*

**Paul**    Please leave us alone.

**Helen**    You keep doing that. Trying to get rid of me. But I have feelings, I take up space, I breathe air. I live, Paul. There's nothing you can do about that.

**Paul**    I know. I'm not saying . . . Helen, I want you to get on with your life too.

**Helen**    But I can't. Not yet.

**Paul**    Why not?

**Helen**   Not until you talk to me.

**Paul**   Talk, what do you even . . . I can't talk to you here.
I'm not . . .

*He looks back to the house.*

If she saw us out here now . . .

**Helen**   You know what, this isn't about her. For once. About
what she thinks, what she feels, what she fucking . . . This is
about me. What I need. I can't sleep, I can't, stop thinking. I
just go over and over and over . . .

*Beat.*

I want to go. Trust me, I don't want to be stood here in the
dark, in the, the . . . I want to get back in my car and I want
to leave this place and never see you again. I promise you
that. But I can't. Not until /

**Paul**   / What? What do you, what could you, possibly want
to talk to me about? Do you need help? Money? Is it money
you need?

*Beat.*

What? What are you, what's that look for? What does
that mean?

**Helen**   I don't want your money, Paul. I don't want
money. Fuck.

**Paul**   No. No, I'm sorry, I just . . .

**Helen**   Christ, you're such a fuck.

**Paul**   I know I am. I'm trying. I'm trying not to be.

**Helen**   Why are you so scared of talking, Paul? To anyone?
What are you hiding?

**Paul**   I'm not. I'm not hiding anything.

*Beat.*

What is it? What do you want to know?

**Helen**   You said something to me. And I need to know if you meant it. I need to know if you were lying. Lying to me, or lying to her.

**Paul**   Helen, I don't know why this is . . .

**Helen**   Because it matters to me.

**Paul**   But why does the, the . . . It's raking. I don't think it's good to rake.

**Helen**   Paul.

**Paul**   We need to, all of us, to, to move forward.

**Helen**   Were you lying, Paul?

*Pause.*

**Paul**   I answer this and, and you go away?

**Helen**   Yes.

**Paul**   Forever?

**Helen**   I, I'll go. I just need to know.

**Paul**   Ok. Ok, then no. I wasn't lying.

**Helen**   To who?

## Day Two

**Four**

*Morning.*

*The sound of birds.*

**Rebecca**'s *bedroom.*

*The sound of a running shower.*

*A knock.*

*Beat.*

*A knock.*

**Paul** *enters, tentatively.*

**Paul**   Hello? Rebecca?

*He hears the shower.*

(*Towards the bathroom.*) Uh, hey Rebecca. Morning. I've, uh, I've put the coffee on.

*He waits, no response.*

*He steps further in.*

I was wondering if you, uh. What you wanted to do today. I thought we could go for a walk? Up the, the mountain? Clear our heads, or . . .?

*Still no response.*

*He steps further in.*

I'll, uh. I'll, I'll just go pour the coffee. (*Louder.*) I've put some coffee on, Helen. Downstairs!

*He realises what he's said.*

*He could eat his face off.*

*He waits. Listening. Carefully.*

Rebecca?

*Just the running shower.*

I, I, I, I didn't mean . . . Rebecca, I'm sorry. I . . .

*He goes to exit, out of the room.*

**Rebecca** *is stood at the door to the hallway.*

**Rebecca**    Paul?

*He jumps.*

**Paul**    *Rebecca.*

**Rebecca**    Are you ok?

**Paul**    I, I thought you were in the shower.

*She hears the shower too.*

**Rebecca**    No?

*She goes into the bathroom.*

*The sound of the shower being switched off.*

*She enters.*

Was it just running like that?

**Paul**    Yeah. I thought you were in there.

**Rebecca**    Oh shit, no. I was /

**Paul**    / You didn't hear me?

**Rebecca**    I was downstairs. I went to dry my towel in the garden.

**Paul**    Oh. Oh, right.

**Rebecca**    I swear I turned it off.

**Paul**    Huh.

**Rebecca**    Maybe there's something wrong with the . . .

**Paul**   Yeah.

**Rebecca**   It's a good job you heard.

**Paul**   What?

**Rebecca**   It's a good job you heard it. It could have flooded the whole fucking house.

**Paul**   Yeah.

**Rebecca**   I should call them. Let them know. Maybe I won't use it, now. Can I share yours?

**Paul**   Course. Yeah, course.

**Rebecca**   Thanks.

*Beat.*

So what was it that you said?

*He looks to the grate.*

*He turns back to her.*

**Paul**   I, uh. I came to tell you that I put coffee on. I put the coffee on. By the way. How did you sleep?

**Rebecca**   I'll be down now. Thanks.

**Five**

*Evening.*

*The kitchen.*

**Paul** *and* **Rebecca** *are sat.*

**Paul**   I wonder what they do.

**Rebecca**   Who?

**Paul**   Next door. I wonder what they do. It's going to be pretty niche if you're able to do it out here.

*Beat.*

**Rebecca**    Maybe they're retired.

**Paul**    Retired?

**Rebecca**    Yeah.

*Beat.*

**Paul**    Well, what about in the winter?

**Rebecca**    What about it?

**Paul**    Can you imagine? It's cold now. And we're only at the, the end of the season. The winter, out here? No, that's . . . It's tough.

**Rebecca**    Yeah. I suppose. I didn't think.

**Paul**    Just the, the. Just the maintenance of it. You know?

**Rebecca**    Hmm.

*Beat.*

I suppose I just like the idea of it. I don't know. Maybe I'm romantic. But the, the, the idea of getting old out somewhere like this. Out in the country. With chickens and rivers and . . .

*Beat.*

I'm sure you're right. I'm sure the reality is much harder.

**Paul**    Hmm, yeah. I imagine places like this. As beautiful as they are. Can turn pretty quickly. You know?

*Beat.*

**Rebecca**    I sometimes think that we're being watched.

**Paul**    What?

**Rebecca**    Not in a bad way. I just, when we're at the window.

**Paul**    What are you talking about?

**Rebecca**   The birds and the . . . Wondering who we are.
Strangers. Course we must make a difference. Suddenly
people turn up. Must notice us about the place.

**Paul**   Oh. Right. Yeah. Well, you know what, they probably,
in the holidays they must get a lot of . . . Hey, we never made
it up the mountain today. Maybe tomorrow we should /

*/ The telephone starts ringing in the hall.*

*They look to each other.*

*She exits, to the phone.*

**Rebecca** (*off, on the phone*)   Hello?

*Beat.*

Who?

*Beat.*

A, uh. A few days.

*Beat.*

No. No, he didn't say.

**Paul** *looks.*

**Rebecca**   I, I don't understand.

*Beat.*

Who did you say you were again?

*Beat.*

Right.

*Pause.*

**Rebecca** *enters.*

*She looks at him.*

*Beat.*

**Paul**   Who was it?

**Rebecca**    No one.

**Paul**    No one? Ha.

**Rebecca** *sits.*

Didn't, uh . . . Didn't sound like no one.

**Rebecca**    What?

**Paul**    It didn't sound like no one.

*Beat.*

So, uh . . .

**Rebecca**    Who do you think it was?

**Paul**    I don't know.

**Rebecca**    Guess.

**Paul**    I, uh /

**Rebecca**    / Buzzzzzzzzzzzzzz.

**Paul**    What?

**Rebecca**    Guess who it was. That's your clue. Buzzzzzzzzzz.

**Paul**    Rebecca, what are you, I don't . . .

**Rebecca**    That's your clue.

**Paul**    A clue?

**Rebecca**    Buzzzzzzzzzz. Come on, guess.

**Paul**    Can you stop doing that?

**Rebecca**    Then guess.

**Paul**    I don't know. A beekeeper?

**Rebecca**    What, no. It was the council.

**Paul**    The what?

**Rebecca**    The council. Giving notice, they're going to be sawing down some trees. Starting tomorrow. Apparently we should have been told.

**Paul**    Oh. Right.

**Rebecca**    That's what the buzzing was. Me cutting down trees.

**Paul**    Oh. Yeah. I see.

**Rebecca**    Buzzzz.

**Paul**    Yeah.

*Beat.*

**Rebecca**    What's with the face?

**Paul**    What face? I don't have a . . .

*Beat.*

**Rebecca**    Who did you think it was?

**Paul**    I said I don't know.

*Pause.*

**Rebecca**    Can I ask you a question?

**Paul**    A question? Uh, yeah, yeah sure. Yeah, I . . .

**Rebecca**    Do you still think about her?

**Paul**    Think about who?

*Beat.*

No. I, no. Jesus. No. Where the fuck did . . .

**Rebecca**    Sorry.

**Paul**    No, I just . . .

**Rebecca**    Was it wrong to ask? I don't know.

**Paul**    No.

**Rebecca**   I mean it must be hard for you. I know that.

**Paul**   No. It's not . . . No.

**Rebecca**   I, I think about her all the time. Well, not her. It. I think about it. And it sits there, this thought, and, and it has a nerve in everything. And I wince every time it's touched.

*Beat.*

What do I do about that, Paul? What do I do?

**Paul**   I don't know.

**Rebecca**   You want to say forget it. You want to say just forget it, please, just let it go, *fuck*. And I wish I could too. For both of us.

**Paul**   I don't want you to forget.

**Rebecca**   No?

**Paul**   No. Because I, I believe that the *us* that overcomes this, is a stronger *us* than if we didn't have to overcome anything at all. I . . .

*Beat.*

**Rebecca**   So you did it for us.

**Paul**   What? No.

**Rebecca**   Because that's what *that* sounds like. Stronger than if we didn't have to, whatever.

**Paul**   No. Then, then I said it wrong. That's not what I meant.

**Rebecca**   No. I know.

**Paul**   Rebecca.

**Rebecca**   No. I know you didn't. I don't know why I did that. I don't know why I do it. I didn't . . .

*Beat.*

Your face, as I came off the phone. I'm sorry. You're on edge all the time.

**Paul**   No. I'm not. I'm . . .

*Pause.*

**Rebecca**   Do you remember Chris Lennon's leaving party, and that fat man who started choking, hacking up those peanuts or whatever.

**Paul**   Uh. I, yeah. Yeah, I'd forgotten about that.

**Rebecca**   And you stepped in and begun thumping his back, really thumping.

**Paul**   Yeah, what, what are, why are you . . .?

**Rebecca**   You were so scared.

**Paul**   I wasn't scared.

**Rebecca**   No, maybe not scared. But you were reluctant, to put yourself in there. In that position. But you did it.

*Beat.*

That's the face you've got on you now. You're putting yourself somewhere where you don't want to be.

**Paul**   Rebecca. I want to be here. I, I want to be here. On a mountain. In a forest. In a house. Just, just me and you.

*Beat.*

*He goes to her.*

*Something has caught her eye in the window.*

What, what is it?

**Rebecca**   No, I just. The light. The outside light.

**Paul**   What?

**Rebecca**   Just flickered on.

**Paul**   It's broken.

**Rebecca**   Is it?

**Paul**   I forgot to say.

**Rebecca**   Oh.

**Paul**   But I'll fix it. It's fine. I'll fix it, Rebecca.

## Six

*Night.*

*Outside the wood shed.*

**Helen** *lingers, half in the shadows.*

## Day Three

**Seven**

*Morning.*

*The mountain.*

**Paul** *and* **Rebecca** *make it to the summit.*

*They are both tired, but his feet are very sore.*

**Paul**   Wow.

**Rebecca**   Yeah.

**Paul**   Just . . . wow.

*She sits.*

You don't get this at home. Do you?

**Rebecca**   No.

**Paul**   You can see for miles.

**Rebecca**   Yeah.

**Paul**   That's probably, I don't know, fifty miles. Easy.

*He sits too.*

Ah.

**Rebecca**   Are you ok?

**Paul**   Yeah, just these, uh . . . These trainers. You know?

**Rebecca**   Yeah.

**Paul**   Maybe I can buy some boots or something.

**Rebecca**   Yeah.

**Paul**   Lucky, that you had a pair of, uh . . .

*Beat.*

Have you ever seen fifty miles before? Just straight on like
that? Well, probably. But not recently. Not in fucking, not
at home.

**Rebecca**    Yeah. No, I haven't.

**Paul**    Yeah.

*Beat.*

I think that's the house. Over there. There's a gap, a bit of a
gap in those trees. Can you see it? I think that's where your,
your light gets through.

**Rebecca**    Yeah.

**Paul**    When it's, uh . . .

**Rebecca**    When there's a sun.

**Paul**    Yeah.

*Beat.*

Let me know when you want those sandwiches, by the way.
Let me know when you want, uh . . . And I'll, I'll make a . . .
Yeah.

*Beat.*

Are you ok?

**Rebecca**    Yeah. Yes. I'm. I'm slightly overwhelmed, Paul.

**Paul**    Oh.

**Rebecca**    But in a good way. I've just suddenly had this
rush of . . .

**Paul**    What?

*Beat.*

**Rebecca**    You know, the air. The fresh air. The way it hits
you. It can (*gestures being wiped out*).

*Beat.*

**Paul**    Yeah I think I'm feeling it too.

*Silence.*

**Rebecca**    Do you remember, the picture my parents had up in their toilet? The downstairs toilet?

**Paul**    Oh. Yeah.

**Rebecca**    Do you remember it?

**Paul**    Yeah.

**Rebecca**    The kind of colours of that. That's this.

*Beat.*

**Paul**    Wasn't that . . .

**Rebecca**    A boat at sea. It was a painting of a boat at sea, yeah. But I mean the colours. I mean the darkness of the trees and the, the grey white of the sky. The ripples of the waves being the tops of the trees.

**Paul**    Yeah.

*Beat.*

**Rebecca**    And that makes me the boat. I suppose. If you follow that through.

*Beat.*

**Paul**    Us.

**Rebecca**    What?

**Paul**    Us. We're the boat.

**Rebecca**    Oh. Yeah. That's what I mean.

*Beat.*

**Paul**    It's not what you said.

**Rebecca**    What?

**Paul**    It's not, uh . . . You didn't say us. You said you.

**Rebecca**    I don't . . .

**Paul**    I wonder. Rebecca. Whether you, whether you . . . It sounds like, it sometimes feels like, you, you . . . You sometimes have a look in your eye. Like it, like you're not really, like I'm . . . Like you're on your own. Like you're so deep in whatever thought or, or . . . You know we sometimes sit in silence for hours. For . . . And I don't even know if you notice it.

*Beat.*

**Rebecca**    I've just been working things out.

**Paul**    No. I know. Of course. I know that.

**Rebecca**    It seems simpler, though. Here.

**Paul**    What, away?

**Rebecca**    Yeah. No. I mean here. Up here.

*Something has caught her eye in the distance. She doesn't take her eyes off it for the rest of the scene.*

I think I know what I need now, Paul.

**Paul**    Yeah?

**Rebecca**    Yes.

*Beat.*

**Paul**    What? What is it? Anything.

**Rebecca**    I think I need fairness.

**Paul**    Yes. Absolutely. Of course. What do you mean?

**Rebecca**    I need fairness in, in . . . pain.

**Paul**    Right.

**Rebecca**    In, yes, pain.

**Paul**    What do you, what does that . . .

**Rebecca**    You hurt me, Paul. And, and I need you to feel that. So you know. What it is, what it does to you. I need you to feel it back. So we can understand each other.

**Paul**    Right.

**Rebecca**    Do you see what I mean?

**Paul**    I, uh, I think so.

**Rebecca**    I need you to bleed. To see you bleeding. But, but I also want that bleeding to stop. See, I want us to heal. Together. That's what I mean. And I think we can only heal if we're both hurt.

*Beat.*

But I understand if that's too much.

*He turns to her.*

**Paul**    No. Rebecca, no. Anything. Anything. I swear.


**Eight**

*Afternoon.*

*Outside the wood shed.*

*The splitting sound of sawing trees.*

**Rebecca** *approaches from the house.*

**Paul** *enters from the shed.*

**Rebecca**    Hey. You're out here.

**Paul**    Hey.

*He is bitten. He slaps his arm.*

**Rebecca**    The noise.

**Paul**    I know, right.

*He is bitten again. He slaps his neck.*

How long did they say they'll be here for?

**Rebecca**   A few days.

**Paul**   So for as long as we are.

**Rebecca**   It might not take that long.

*He walks across the space. He limps. For the rest of the play he moves quite gingerly on his feet.*

**Rebecca**   How are your feet?

**Paul**   Yeah, no. I'll be fine. I've just, they'll just blister up. My own fault for not packing proper . . . I'll just buy some.

*He slaps his neck again.*

**Rebecca**   Are you ok?

**Paul**   Yeah, I just think they've, I don't know. Are you getting bitten?

**Rebecca**   No.

**Paul**   I think it's . . . They're biting to shit.

**Rebecca**   Who?

**Paul**   *Who.* The flies. Big gnats. I think they've kicked up the nests or something. I'm being chewed up.

**Rebecca**   Yeah. Weird. I'm not . . .

**Paul**   Maybe it's my sweat.

*He slaps his neck.*

Or something.

**Rebecca**   Do you need a hand?

**Paul**   No. No, I was just, getting some logs in for the night.

**Rebecca**   I've some coffee on. I was coming out to say.

*He scratches his hand.*

**Paul**   Oh great. I was gonna . . . When I came back in.

**Rebecca**   I just . . .

**Paul**   No. Yeah. Thanks.

**Rebecca**   Great. Ok. I'll . . .

**Paul**   Hey. Do you, uh, do you know what, what's happened to the axe?

**Rebecca**   The . . . No?

**Paul**   It's not in the shed.

**Rebecca**   It's not?

**Paul**   No.

**Rebecca**   Weird.

**Paul**   It was just hanging up in the . . .

*He slaps his neck.*

Jesus Christ, these bastards.

**Rebecca**   Did you need it?

**Paul**   Huh?

**Rebecca**   Do you need the axe?

**Paul**   Well no. I just . . . I noticed it wasn't there.

**Rebecca**   Huh.

**Paul**   It's less of a need for it and more that, you know, it's been moved or, or stolen.

**Rebecca**   Stolen?

**Paul**   I don't know.

**Rebecca**   Don't you lock the shed?

**Paul**   Yeah.

**Rebecca**   Did you lock it last night?

**Paul**   Yeah, I did. I remember.

**Rebecca**   Doesn't look broken into.

**Paul**    No.

**Rebecca**    Maybe you moved it and forgot where you moved it to.

**Paul**    I, I don't think I moved it.

**Rebecca**    Think?

**Paul**    Why would I move it?

**Rebecca**    I don't know.

**Paul**    Well I didn't. Maybe they broke into the back. I'll look round the . . .

**Rebecca**    Who?

**Paul**    Whoever took it.

*He slaps his neck.*

**Rebecca**    Why are you so sure you think someone's taken it?

**Paul**    I don't know. What's the other, you know, what else could have happened? I told you I didn't lose it.

**Rebecca**    I just . . . But who, Paul? Who would take it?

**Paul**    I don't know.

*Beat.*

**Rebecca**    Unless it's the neighbour.

**Paul**    Who, you think?

**Rebecca**    Maybe they have a key and borrowed it.

**Paul**    You think?

**Rebecca**    Maybe.

*Beat.*

Maybe you can go and ask them. If you're worried.

*He slaps his neck again.*

*She goes to leave.*

**Paul**   Uh . . . So, uh, I have to tell you something, Rebecca.

*Beat.*

**Rebecca**   What is it, Paul?

**Paul**   I, I . . . the note. That they said they'd leave, that they . . . uh, left. There was a, it was in the kitchen. And, I, uh . . .

*He slaps his neck.*

I didn't throw it away on purpose. I, uh . . .

*He exhales.*

I didn't think anything of it. I just saw it and I thought it was just a generic, like . . . and, and by the time I realised what I'd done, when you said about the directions and the, the . . .

*He slaps his arm.*

*She watches his hands.*

I, I felt like too much of an idiot, so I didn't say. I should have told you but I didn't say.

*He scratches his hand.*

Rebecca.

*Beat.*

**Rebecca**   Ok.

**Paul**   It's not ok.

*Beat.*

I'm sorry.

**Rebecca**   It's ok.

**Paul**   You don't have to say that.

**Rebecca**   Then what do you want me to say?

**Paul**   I don't know. It just feels like it needs to be acknowledged.

**Rebecca**   Acknowledged.

**Paul**   Yeah. I, I feel like I've let you down. Again.

*Beat.*

**Rebecca**   Thank you for telling me, Paul.


**Nine**

*Afternoon.*

**Rebecca** *is in the kitchen.*

**Paul** *enters from outside.*

**Paul**   Ah fuck. Rebecca?

**Rebecca**   What's wrong?

**Paul**   A fucking, a splinter.

**Rebecca**   A what?

**Paul**   A splinter. Look.

*She looks at his hand.*

*She stares.*

Rebecca?

*She keeps staring.*

Rebecca?

**Rebecca**   Oh. Sorry. Yeah. It's a . . . It's a big one.

**Paul**   It hurts, it's . . . Do we have any tweezers?

**Rebecca**   No.

**Paul**   Shit.

**Rebecca**   I can get it out. Though.

**Paul**    Really?

**Rebecca**    Yeah.

**Paul**    What with?

**Rebecca**    My fingers.

**Paul**    Your fingers?

**Rebecca**    Yeah, I'll just . . . (*She motions pinching.*)

**Paul**    Oh God.

**Rebecca**    You'll be fine. I've got sharp nails. It'll just . . .
What?

**Paul**    Nothing.

**Rebecca**    It'll be fine.

*Beat.*

I mean, what else are you going to do?

*Beat.*

**Paul**    Ok.

**Rebecca**    We'll do it here.

**Paul**    Here?

**Rebecca**    In the light. I need to see it.

**Paul**    No. Yeah. Sure.

*He offers his hand.*

*She takes it.*

Be gentle, yeah? Be /

/ *She squeezes his hand.*

Oh God.

**Rebecca**    Hang on.

*She squeezes more.*

**Paul**    Fuck, *Rebecca.*

*She looks him in the eye.*

**Rebecca**    I'm doing it.

*She squeezes.*

*He is almost doubled over.*

**Paul**    I don't think . . . I don't think it's coming . . .

**Rebecca**    It is.

**Paul**    *Please*!

*He tries to pull his hand away. She doesn't let go.*

Please, it's, it's bleeding.

**Rebecca**    It's almost there.

**Paul**    Christ . . .

**Rebecca**    It's . . .

*He pulls.*

*She lets go.*

*He clutches the palm of his hand.*

*Silence, apart from their heavy breathing (**Paul**, in pain; **Rebecca**, something else).*

*She looks at the splinter between her fingers.*

There.

**Paul**    Rebecca.

**Rebecca**    There. We got it.

**Paul**    Rebecca, what the fuck?

**Rebecca**    Do you need, like, a bandage or a plaster or something?

**Paul**    Uh. Yeah. Do we . . .

**Rebecca**   No. I can pick something up in the village though.

**Paul**   The village?

**Rebecca**   Yeah.

**Paul**   You'll pick something up in the village?

**Rebecca**   Yeah, I can drive over.

**Paul**   What, we couldn't pick up some fucking tweezers in the village?

**Rebecca**   No. I, I wanted to /

**Paul**   / Christ.

**Rebecca**   You need to get that kind of shit out as quick as you can. For, for infections and whatever.

*Beat.*

Paul.

**Paul**   No. Yeah. Sure. I'm just . . .

*She examines his hand.*

I mean you took half my fucking palm with it. I'm like . . .

*He shows her.*

Fucking stigmata.

**Rebecca**   Run it under the tap. I'll go and get a towel or something, for now.

*She goes to leave.*

*He tastes the blood on his hand. It catches her eye.*

By the way. Uh. Don't worry about the note, Paul. It's fine now.

*She exits.*

*He watches her leave.*

**Ten**

*Afternoon.*

**Paul** *is feeling the bandage on his hand.*

**Rebecca** *enters.*

*He notices her watching.*

**Paul**   Oh hey.

**Rebecca**   How are you doing?

**Paul**   Yeah, just . . . Yeah, just wonder how tight it should be. Whether I've got it on too tight.

*She steps forward.*

**Rebecca**   It looks ok to me.

**Paul**   You think?

**Rebecca**   Yeah. You've done it well. Really well, actually.

**Paul**   Thanks. I didn't really know what I was doing.

**Rebecca**   You managed to do that on your own like that?

**Paul**   Yeah, I just . . .

**Rebecca**   Impressive.

**Paul**   No.

**Rebecca**   One handed and all.

*Beat.*

**Paul**   I, I, I just wrapped it.

**Rebecca**   Huh.

*Beat.*

You know you could have asked for my help.

**Paul**   No. Oh, I know. Thank you.

**Rebecca**   If I knew you were doing it now.

**Paul**   I just thought I'd get it done.

*He shows his hand.*

Sorted.

**Rebecca**   Ok.

**Paul**   But, you know, I'll need help. To, to change it. When I have to change it.

**Rebecca**   Sure, well maybe.

**Paul**   No. I'm sure.

**Rebecca**   You did that pretty fine on your own.


**Eleven**

*Evening.*

*The kitchen.*

*A scream.*

**Paul** *rushes in from outside.*

**Rebecca** *darts in from the living room.*

*He notices the patch of blood on her shirt.*

**Paul**   Rebecca, fuck. What's, what's /

/ *He rushes to her. She stops him.*

**Rebecca**   No.

**Paul**   What's happened?

**Rebecca**   There's a . . .

**Paul**   A what?

*He heads to the living room.*

**Rebecca**   No. Don't. There's a, a bird. Some kind of, I don't know, a bird.

**Paul**   A bird?

**Rebecca**   Yeah.

**Paul**   In the house?

**Rebecca**   In the living room.

**Paul**   Fuck.

**Rebecca**   I was just sat there, reading, and, and I could just feel these eyes on me.

**Paul**   Eyes?

**Rebecca**   And then it just . . . landed on me.

**Paul**   Landed on you? From through the window?

**Rebecca**   And, and I, I, I shot up. I shot up and it rolled off me and fell on the floor and just, just sat there.

**Paul**   Sat there? So it's, it's dead?

**Rebecca**   It's black and greasy and, and . . . It was really crying out, really scrawing.

**Paul**   But is it dead now? Rebecca?

**Rebecca**   I don't know. It should be.

**Paul**   Ok. Well, I'll, I'll handle it.

**Rebecca**   What are you going to do?

**Paul**   I'm going to get it out.

**Rebecca**   How?

**Paul**   I don't know. With a, a, a bucket. There's a bucket in the wood shed.

*He goes to exit outside.*

*He has a better idea.*

No. No, a, a blanket. Is there a blanket or a, a sheet or something, I can wrap it up.

**Rebecca**   There's a throw. On the sofa. In there.

**Paul**   Right. Ok. Well I'll use that.

*He inhales, and exits.*

**Rebecca**   Be careful.

*She stands away.*

*Pause.*

**Paul** *enters.*

**Paul**   It's uh, yeah it's dead.

**Rebecca**   Ok.

**Paul**   So I'm going to, I'm going to take it out the back.

**Rebecca**   What for?

**Paul**   To bury it.

**Rebecca**   Oh. Right. Tonight?

**Paul**   No, maybe in the, in the morning. Because it'll have to be, uh, deep enough so the foxes don't get at it.

**Rebecca**   Oh right. Yeah.

**Paul**   Otherwise they'll just spend the whole week digging it up.

**Rebecca**   Right.

**Paul**   I can just put it in the shed until morning.

*Beat.*

**Rebecca**   Paul /

**Paul**   / It was really, you know, chewed up. It was . . . Whatever had got at it had really . . .

**Rebecca**   What do you mean got at it?

**Paul**   It was like, half eaten.

**Rebecca** Oh. Shit. Right.

*Beat.*

**Paul** Anyway, I'll clear it while you change.

**Rebecca** Change?

**Paul** Yeah, your . . .

*She notices that her top has a large patch of blood on it.*

**Rebecca** Oh God.

**Paul** Yeah.

**Rebecca** That's so gross.

**Paul** Yeah.

**Rebecca** We need to clean everything.

**Paul** Yeah, that's ok.

**Rebecca** Ok. Well. I'll go and, uh, shower.

**Paul** Sure.

*She exits.*

*Beat.*

*He listens to her walking up the stairs.*

*He looks up to the grate.*


**Twelve**

*Night.*

*Outside the wood shed.*

*Darkness.*

*The light sensor is flickering.*

**Paul** *is stood, with the torch, looking at it.*

**Helen** *comes and stands in the way.*

*He jumps out of his skin.*

**Paul**   Oh Jesus.

**Helen**   Need a hand?

*She steps out of the torch light.*

**Paul**   I, I . . . You shouldn't do that.

**Helen**   It might be damp. Getting into the fuse.

**Paul**   Yeah, that's what I thought. I dried it but it's still getting wet.

*Beat.*

She thinks someone's here.

**Helen**   They are.

**Paul**   But she knows, Helen.

**Helen**   You just said she thinks.

**Paul**   Please. Come on. I've answered every question you've asked.

**Helen**   Bar one.

**Paul**   Every reasonable question. And, and you've been smoking. She'll smell it and she'll think it's me.

**Helen**   So she made you quit?

**Paul**   No. She didn't make me. She actually, she actually said I could smoke if I wanted to.

**Helen**   Generous.

**Paul**   Stop it.

*Beat.*

I'm worried about you, you know. Doing this. I don't, and it's not for me that I'm saying this, I genuinely don't think it's healthy. To be lingering.

**Helen**   It's the most honest we've ever been.

**Paul**   It's not right, Helen.

**Helen**   You're getting somewhere though. *It's not for me that I'm saying this.* It's almost as though you're starting to care about others.

**Paul**   I've always, I do care. That's my problem. I care too much.

**Helen**   Yeah. No, you're probably right.

**Paul**   I want you to go home, Helen. I don't want this for you. This could end badly. Really badly. I don't want that. No one does.

**Helen**   We're just talking.

**Paul**   You've been watching.

**Helen**   No, I haven't.

**Paul**   You have. I know. I've, I don't know, I've, I've felt it.

**Helen**   Felt?

**Paul**   I can tell. And, and she's felt it too. It's dangerous, it's . . .

**Helen**   Then why don't you just tell her?

**Paul**   Tell her what?

**Helen**   That you've seen me.

**Paul**   Can you imagine?

**Helen**   I mean, *you* haven't done anything wrong. Have you? I've just, I'm the one that's putting us here.

*He scratches his hand.*

**Paul**   Hey, you've not . . .

**Helen**   What?

**Paul**   Listen, you have to tell me the truth now.

**Helen**   What is it, Paul?

**Paul**   You've not been . . . messing with stuff. Have you?

**Helen**   Messing?

**Paul**   You've not been . . .

**Helen**   I've never come near you. Both. If that's what you're asking.

**Paul**   Ok.

**Helen**   I've not.

**Paul**   No. Ok.

**Helen**   Why?

*Beat.*

**Paul**   Things are just getting, there have been moments, of . . . You know, it would be a really good idea if you left.

**Helen**   Then answer the last question.

**Paul**   No.

**Helen**   Paul.

**Paul**   You can't, you don't want me to, Helen.

**Helen**   Come on. Tell me. If you had met me first, would we /

**Paul**   / It's not fair.

**Helen**   On who?

*Pause.*

**Paul**   I should probably go back in. Will you drive home safe? Tonight?

**Helen**    She's making you feel guilty.

**Paul**    She's not making me feel anything.

**Helen**    She's punishing you.

**Paul**    I, hey, no. I did, we did a bad thing and, and this? I'm fucking grateful that I still have a chance. I'm grateful that, that . . .

**Helen**    She's hurting you and she's making you think that's right. It's not right, Paul. She thinks it's helping her but it doesn't make her any better. It's just tonguing a sore. She's just fucking /

**Paul**    / Right. Now you've, you've overstepped a mark.

**Helen**    Paul.

**Paul**    I mean, there have been marks you've overstepped, you've jumped a lot of marks the past couple of days, but now, now it's . . . I think it's time to go.

*He tries to guide her away.*

**Helen**    I'm not going to punish you for your mistakes, Paul. I'm not going to hurt you because I hurt.

**Paul**    Go now, before one of us says something that /

**Helen**    / Come with me.

**Paul**    What?

**Helen**    I'll go. But come with me, Paul. There's no need to suffer like this. A fresh start.

**Paul**    No.

**Helen**    A clean slate.

**Paul**    No.

**Helen**    Why not?

**Paul**    *Why not*, I can't.

**Helen**   Why not?

**Paul**   I don't want to.

*Beat.*

**Helen**   That's not true.

**Paul**   It's . . . I believe it, with every . . .

*He scratches his hand.*

With everything. I believe it. I know it.

**Helen**   Are you happy?

**Paul**   Yes.

**Helen**   Are you happy here?

**Paul**   Yes.

**Helen**   No, you're not.

**Paul**   Helen.

**Helen**   I can see it. I can always tell with you.

**Paul**   Hey. No. Now, stop it.

**Helen**   You can't lie to me.

**Paul**   Stop it.

*Beat.*

**Helen**   There's nothing keeping *you* here other than guilt. And *she's* only here because she feels you owe her something, waiting for you to pay her back. That's not a relationship.

**Paul**   Don't say that.

*He looks back to the house.*

**Helen**   It's just weird. You don't even like each other anymore.

**Paul**   You don't understand us.

**Helen**    All I see is like, genuine distain.

**Paul**    You have to go now, Helen. It's time, you really have to leave.

**Helen**    Both of us. Leave now. Me and you, Paul. We could go anywhere.

**Paul**    No.

**Helen**    We could be so happy.

*Beat.*

**Paul**    I'm staying here. Go, Helen. For Christ sake, let us just get on with our lives. I'm not /

**Helen**    / Didn't you hear what I /

**Paul**    / I'm not talking to you anymore.

**Helen**    But /

*She moves towards him. She reaches out to him.*

**Paul**    / Just go!

*He pushes her away. Harder than he means to. She slips and falls.*

*He goes to help her, but holds back.*

Leave me alone, Helen. Leave us both alone. Please. I . . . Will you? I, I won't ask again.

*The light flickers as she exits.*

*He watches.*

*The light cuts out completely.*

*He turns on the torch.*

# Day Four

**Thirteen**

*Morning.*

*The kitchen.*

**Paul** *is sat.*

**Rebecca** *enters.*

**Paul**   Hey.

**Rebecca**   Hey. Morning.

*He stands.*

**Paul**   I put the coffee on.

**Rebecca**   Thanks.

**Paul**   A few hours ago.

**Rebecca**   Oh.

**Paul**   I can make fresh.

**Rebecca**   No, I'll do it.

**Paul**   No. It's ok, I just . . .

**Rebecca**   I'm sorry I slept in. Have you been waiting?

*Beat.*

You should have knocked. You could have knocked.

**Paul**   I did.

**Rebecca**   Oh.

**Paul**   But it's fine. It's, you know. It's good to be, uh. I'm glad you're sleeping much better.

**Rebecca**   It's been so odd, the past couple of days. I've slept like . . . And I've been having the most vivid dreams.

**Paul**    Oh, yeah?

**Rebecca**    I, I went to Rome. Last night. Can you believe
that? I was in Rome.

**Paul**    How do you know it was Rome? We've never been
to Rome.

**Rebecca**    No, I just . . . Well, I suppose I just knew.

**Paul**    Was I there?

*Beat.*

**Rebecca**    Yes.

**Paul**    No, I wasn't.

**Rebecca**    Maybe. No, I don't . . . I don't remember so well.

**Paul**    Ok.

**Rebecca**    But I mean, you probably were.

**Paul**    What did you, uh. What did you do then, in Rome?

*Beat.*

**Rebecca**    You were making breakfast.

**Paul**    No.

**Rebecca**    I'm sorry.

**Paul**    Don't worry about it.

**Rebecca**    You were going to do your eggs.

**Paul**    I can do it tomorrow. It's fine.

**Rebecca**    I'm sorry, Paul.

**Paul**    I wasn't, I wasn't so much in the . . . It'll keep. I'm
not, like. It's not a waste.

**Rebecca**    No.

*Beat.*

I feel bad, though.

**Paul**   You went to Rome!

*He exits.*

*Beat.*

*The coffee percolator is turned on. It slowly bubbles over the next couple of minutes.*

*He returns. He's playing with the plaster on his hand.*

**Rebecca**   So what have you been up to?

**Paul**   What have I been up to? I don't know. Not much. I suppose you heard.

**Rebecca**   No. Actually.

**Paul**   I was going to bury that bird. This morning.

**Rebecca**   Great. Good idea.

**Paul**   Yeah. Get rid of it.

**Rebecca**   Yeah.

*Beat.*

**Paul**   You know, it's funny. I was going through it, in, in my head, the whole bird thing.

**Rebecca**   Oh yeah. Weird. What a weird . . .

**Paul**   Yeah, it was weird. It, it . . . I can imagine the shock.

**Rebecca**   Yeah.

**Paul**   For it to just fall in on, on you like that.

**Rebecca**   Yeah.

*Beat.*

**Paul**   And, and the . . . The calling out. The blood, the scrawing. I can imagine that's quite traumatic, with the . . . And, uh. To shut the window and then come and find me.

*Beat.*

Because that's what, that's what happened, right? The, the window?

**Rebecca**    I don't . . .

**Paul**    You shut the window? Before you came out? Or did you leave it open?

**Rebecca**    I don't remember, Paul.

**Paul**    Oh.

**Rebecca**    It was all so quick.

**Paul**    Yeah, no. I just.

*Beat.*

The window was closed, Rebecca. When I went in there. It wasn't open.

*Beat.*

**Rebecca**    So I must have shut it then.

**Paul**    Did you?

**Rebecca**    I don't remember.

**Paul**    Yeah. Or.

*Pause.*

**Rebecca**    Or what? Or what, Paul?

*Beat.*

What's going on, Paul?

**Paul**    I don't know. I'm just piecing together, I'm trying to make it make sense just piecing together all the . . . All the information. If that makes sense.

**Rebecca**    Yes.

*Beat.*

**Paul**   You said it should be dead. I asked if the bird was dead and you said that yeah it should be.

*Beat.*

**Rebecca**   I'm sorry that it's confusing.

**Paul**   It's just . . .

**Rebecca**   But I don't know what you want to say. It's just what happened. I can't explain it.

**Paul**   It's what?

**Rebecca**   I said it's just what happened.

*Pause.*

**Paul**   Rebecca, are you . . .

**Rebecca**   You know what, Paul. I appreciate everything that's happening. And I'm grateful for how open and honest you're being.

**Paul**   That's . . .

**Rebecca**   Yeah.

**Paul**   That's ok.

**Rebecca**   Yes. It is.

**Paul**   You know, the, the, your coffee. Will be ready. I'll go and . . .

*He goes to exit.*

**Rebecca**   Thank you. For telling me what you were thinking, Paul. How you were feeling.

**Paul**   Well . . .

**Rebecca**   It's good to know what's going on in there.

*Beat.*

*He goes to exit again.*

You'd tell me. If there was anything else. Wouldn't you, Paul?

**Paul**  Uh, yeah. Yes. Of course.

*Beat.*

So I'll just /

**Rebecca**  / I'd like to go up the mountain. Again. Today. Do you think we can?

**Paul**  Well, I uh. I haven't got, uh. Bought those boots yet.

**Rebecca**  Right.

**Paul**  But I mean, I suppose I could just wear the trainers again. My feet are, are kind of getting better. So I mean.


**Fourteen**

*Afternoon.*

*The mountain.*

**Rebecca** *is stood.*

*The faint sound of cutting trees.*

**Paul** *eventually enters. His feet are screaming in pain.*

**Rebecca**  I wonder, with all their work, how quickly the forest will right itself. How often they have to cut and tear down, and how quickly the forest grows back, and . . .

**Paul**  Trees take a long time to grow. They're, they're, they don't just grow back.

*Beat.*

*He sits. He starts to undo his trainers.*

**Rebecca**  What are you doing?

**Paul**  I just need to . . . My toes are . . . They're just . . .

**Rebecca**   What?

**Paul**   I don't know. Starting to go, going numb.

**Rebecca**   Numb?

**Paul**   I can't feel anything in them.

*Pause.*

**Rebecca**   I sometimes wondered if you were numb.

**Paul** *sighs.*

**Paul**   Do we, do we have to talk now?

**Rebecca**   I wondered if you had to be numb to be able to
. . .

**Paul**   Rebecca, please.

**Rebecca**   Because after, after you'd told me, after I left, I
. . . I don't know. I wondered if I was missing something, if I
just didn't understand. So I went out and I, you know, did it
myself.

**Paul**   What do you mean? Did what?

**Rebecca**   And I found it hard to be able to, I couldn't switch
off, at all. From feeling that /

**Paul**   / Did what yourself, Rebecca?

**Rebecca**   I mean it was a complete fucking car crash. It was
awful. Disgusting, for, for most of it.

*He stands.*

**Paul**   What are you talking about?

**Rebecca**   So, you know, it showed me, it made me think,
that you must have an enormous resilience. Or, or a capacity
for numbness that I . . .

*Beat.*

**Paul**   Rebecca, are you telling me that you slept with someone else?

**Rebecca**   I, yes. But the point I'm /

**Paul**   / But? But the point? The, the point, Rebecca, oh my God, the, the . . . I can't believe you, you didn't fucking tell me.

**Rebecca**   It was once and it was terrible and it was, the reason I'm telling you Paul, is because it's about trying to understand /

**Paul**   / Wait, wait, wait, wait. I, I just . . . You can't . . .

**Rebecca**   I can't what? I can't what, Paul?

**Paul**   Who with?

**Rebecca**   You wouldn't know them.

**Paul**   Who, Rebecca?

**Rebecca**   It doesn't matter who, Paul. You wouldn't know them.

**Paul**   I can't believe, is this true? Are you telling the truth?

**Rebecca**   Do you want proof?

**Paul**   I, no. Jesus. No, I . . .

**Rebecca**   Because I kept the texts, so /

**Paul**   / Don't, don't, don't. Why. Why is this a game to you?

**Rebecca**   It's not a game.

**Paul**   Unless this is like, this is, I mean, who's the, the, I mean, to, to . . .

*He slaps his neck.*

Christ.

*Beat.*

**Rebecca**   Are you angry with me, Paul?

**Paul**   What?

**Rebecca**   Are you angry, now that I've told you that, are you angry with me?

*He swallows the world.*

**Paul**   No.

**Rebecca**   No?

**Paul**   No. How could I be? Because you'd just . . . I'm just shocked, and hurt. Is all.

**Rebecca**   Shocked and hurt.

**Paul**   But I'm not angry.


**Fifteen**

*Afternoon.*

*The kitchen.*

**Rebecca** *and* **Helen** *are together, raucously laughing.*

**Paul** *enters. They don't notice at first.*

*He watches them.*

**Paul**   Rebecca?

**Rebecca**   Oh. Here he is.

**Paul**   Rebecca.

**Rebecca**   God, look at you, Paul. Are you ok?

**Paul**   What's . . . what's happening?

**Rebecca**   Paul's hurt his feet. Were you able to get the trainers off ok?

**Paul**   What, what, what's going on?

*Beat.*

**Rebecca**  Are you ok, Paul?

**Paul**  What's . . . I didn't know.

**Rebecca**  Didn't know what? Paul, this is our neighbour. Heather.

**Paul**  What?

**Rebecca**  We were talking outside, while you were upstairs. I invited her in. That's ok, isn't it?

**Helen**  Nice to meet you.

*She offers a hand.*

Heather.

**Paul** *and* **Helen** *shake hands.*

**Paul**  Uh.

**Rebecca**  I was telling Heather how fascinated we've been with who might live out here. She was telling me she's lived here for forty years.

**Paul**  What?

**Helen**  Me and my husband, George he was called, moved here when there was still the timber mill. It was different then. If you can imagine. Of course you wouldn't get any work out here anymore. Apart from in the holidays.

**Rebecca**  And she was telling me that this place, it used to be a swingers' retreat. Can you believe that?

**Helen**  You'd see some things. I had to persuade them to buy some curtains.

**Rebecca** *and* **Helen** *laugh.*

**Paul**  Rebecca, can I talk to you?

**Rebecca**  We are talking, Paul.

**Paul**  Can I talk to you out there?

**Rebecca**   Don't be rude.

**Rebecca** *turns back to* **Helen**.

**Rebecca**   Please excuse my partner. I think a few days out in the country has turned him feral.

**Helen**   Oh no. I understand. George was the same. He loathed the winters because there'd be no one about and too much alone time drove him crazy. Not everyone can deal with the quiet. Now I've never minded silences myself.

**Rebecca**   It sounds like bliss to me.

**Helen**   And then there was the Dormers. That's the family that lived here before it became a, what do you call it, a resort. They adored it. Especially the quiet times of year. It was as though the Dormers thought that the world would be a fine place, were it not for other people. All they wanted was to be left alone. Well, perhaps not so much the children, but they enjoyed the forest. The loneliness became part of the attraction. Once the mill closed. For people to get out, of their lives, of their world. To run away. It just made it worse for George once he lost the work and he would have wanted to move back, but I never asked him.

*Beat.*

I sometimes wonder what kind of people those Dormer children turned out to be. They liked the fire too.

**Paul**   What?

**Helen**   They used to enjoy feeding the fire.

**Rebecca**   I was telling Heather about your new hobby. What did you call it, a wood eater?

**Paul**   Yeah.

**Helen**   George used to sit for hours at our fire. What goes on in men's minds.

**Rebecca**   I daren't think.

*They both laugh.*

We've solved the axe mystery, by the way.

**Paul**   What?

**Rebecca**   What happened to the axe. We've worked it out. I was right. It was Heather. She borrowed it. She has a key to the wood shed.

*Beat.*

Paul, are you ok?

**Paul** *staggers to the door.*

**Paul**   I, I . . . uh. I need to go out.

**Rebecca**   No, stay.

**Rebecca** *goes to him.*

**Paul**   I'm not, you'll have to excuse me, I'm feeling a bit, need some fresh air.

**Helen**   You could have an infection.

**Paul**   What?

**Helen**   If you're feeling unwell and you've had blisters on your feet, they could have got infected.

**Rebecca**   Oh that's a good point.

**Helen**   Do you have a temperature?

**Paul**   No.

**Helen** *goes to him.*

**Helen**   Well let me check.

**Paul**   No, I'm, I'm . . .

**Rebecca**   You should let her check, Paul.

**Paul**   I'm, I don't want my temperature /

**Paul** *backs away,* **Rebecca** *and* **Helen** *gather around him.*

**Helen**   / You need to be careful with infected blisters, they can wipe you right out.

**Paul**   No. Leave me. Please.

**Rebecca**   Paul.

**Paul**   I'm fine.

**Helen**   Just to see if you're burning up.

**Paul** *breaks away, between them.*

**Paul**   Get off!

*Beat.*

**Rebecca**   Paul.

**Paul**   She's not, she's not who you think she is, Rebecca.

**Helen**   I'm sorry?

**Paul**   What was it? Heather?

**Helen**   Heather.

**Paul**   She doesn't fucking live here.

**Rebecca**   I'm sorry, Heather. I don't know what's got into him.

**Paul**   Stop calling her that. I don't . . . She's making a fool of you.

**Rebecca**   Paul.

**Helen**   I think I should go.

**Paul**   Yes. I think you should. I've asked you to, many times. Too many times. More than I needed to.

**Helen**   I'm sorry?

**Paul**   And I warned you. I fucking warned you.

**Rebecca**   Paul.

**Paul**   But now . . .

**Helen** *backs away.*

**Rebecca**   Paul, what are you doing?

**Paul**   She's . . . She's . . .

**Rebecca**   She's *what*? What?

**Paul** *looks into* **Rebecca**'s *eyes, searching.*

**Paul**   You know what she is. And I asked her, I demanded that she leaves us alone.

**Helen**   I've never met you before in my life.

**Paul**   You're a liar!

**Rebecca**   Paul, calm down.

**Paul**   I don't know what you want from me. I don't know what you're expecting me to do.

**Rebecca**   Who are you talking to, Paul?

**Paul**   But this. All this. It's not my fault, I didn't, I didn't. I didn't.

*He turns to* **Helen**.

**Paul**   Get out. Get out of this house.

**Helen**   I'm sorry, but I don't know what I've /

/ **Paul** *pushes* **Helen** *out through the back door.*

**Paul**   Get out!

**Rebecca**   Paul!

*Silence.*

**Paul**   Who was that, Rebecca?

**Rebecca**   You know who it was.

**Paul**   Say it. Say her name.

**Rebecca**   What?

**Paul**    Say her name. So I know you know.

**Rebecca**    What are you talking about?

**Paul**    Tell me what you're doing to me.

**Rebecca**    Paul, I'm not doing anything to /

**Paul**    / Say it!

*Beat.*

Tell me who that was.

**Rebecca**    That. Was a woman. Called Heather.

**Paul**    No.

**Rebecca**    Who lives next door.

**Paul**    No.

**Rebecca**    And has lived her since 1976.

**Paul**    No, no, no.

**Rebecca**    Her husband is buried in the church down the road.

**Paul**    It's lies, Rebecca. It's all lies.

**Rebecca**    It's not!

**Paul**    It is!

**Rebecca**    Then tell me the truth.

*Beat.*

If that's not who that is, then tell me the truth. Who is it, Paul? Who is it?

*Beat.*

Do you have anything you want to tell me, Paul?

**Paul**    No.

**Rebecca**    Then that, is Heather.

*Beat.*

**Paul**   What you're doing here, what you've done, is nothing like what I did.

**Rebecca**   What?

**Paul**   I mean, whatever you're, you're, you're . . . Whatever this is, whatever you're playing at.

**Rebecca**   What are you talking about?

**Paul**   I could see it in your eyes when you dug out that splinter. The, the way you've kept me walking up and down that fucking mountain. The way you're messing with my head with the bird and the, the lies and the, the and her. Bringing her out here. I mean, that just, can you just, can you tell me what, what all this was meant to, to achieve, other than, than to fuck me up? What does that, how does that even help you?

**Rebecca**   Bring who out here?

*Beat.*

Bring who out here, Paul?

**Paul**   You know you're a terrible, you're a really terrible liar, Rebecca.

*He goes to leave.*

I'll tell you one thing. The, the, the difference. Between this and what I did to. I never intended to hurt you. That's, I never hurt you on purpose. And so this pain, this fucking, it's useless, it doesn't help us one bit. It's torture.

**Rebecca**   That doesn't mean it's useless.

**Paul**   What? You know, I think, I think I have to go home.

**Rebecca**   No.

**Paul**   No? What do you mean no? You can't . . . You can't just say no, Rebecca.

**Rebecca**   But we've still got a day left.

**Sixteen**

*Night.*

*Outside the wood shed.*

*The light is triggered by the sensor.*

**Paul** *is stood.*

**Rebecca** *enters.*

**Paul**   The car's packed. Everything's . . . It's just your bags.

**Rebecca**   It's probably not good to drive at night.

**Paul**   It's fine.

**Rebecca**   And as you say, you haven't been sleeping. So maybe it's better if I drive.

*Beat.*

**Paul**   It's fine.

**Rebecca**   I just wonder why we can't wait until the morning.

**Paul**   We need to get home, we need space, we need to, to . . . And then, we need to talk.

**Rebecca**   We came out here for space, we came out here to talk.

**Paul**   No. One of us did.

*Beat.*

**Rebecca**   Ok. Well, I'll . . .

*She goes to leave, she stops.*

The thing about my pain, Paul. Is that it never stopped. It just dug deeper in. And so while I no longer feel it on my skin, or in my flesh. I feel it in my blood. And in my bones. And in my brain. Suffering like, to re-create, to make fair, it's quite hard to, it's quite hard to find something that never stops, that gets you right down into the roots.

**Paul**   Rebecca . . .

**Rebecca**   You asked me to come here, Paul. And I tried my best to forgive you. But what forgiveness needed was something that we could never have. And that's trust. You've lied and you've lied and so there's nothing. Because of you, inside me there's nothing. And you need to feel what that's like too.

*She exits.*

*The light flickers.*

*It cuts out.*

*Pitch black.*

**Paul**   Shit.

*A time of fumbling.*

*He turns on the torch.*

*It is pitch black other than the single shaft of light emitted by the torch.*

Rebecca!

*There is nothing.*

Rebecca!

*The sound of movement.*

*He looks around. Nothing.*

*A noise. More footsteps.*

*He swivels the torch around.*

*No one.*

Please. I can't see.

*He swivels the torch around.*

*It suddenly shines on* **Helen**'s *face.*

*He screams.*

*He drops the torch.*

*Pitch black.*

*The torch is lit again,* **Paul***'s holding it.*

Where are you? What are you . . .

*Nothing.*

Christ. Oh my God. Please.

*He swivels the torch around.*

I can't . . .

*He falls.*

*He cries out in pain.*

*He drops the torch.*

*He picks up the torch; he's now at ground level.*

I've, I . . . I've fallen. I've . . . Rebecca! My foot. I've . . .

*The torch shines on someone's feet.*

*He points the light up.*

**Helen** *is stood over him.*

*He screams. Drops the torch.*

*Darkness again.*

**Paul***'s cries.*

Rebecca!

*Silence.*

*The torch is lit.*

**Rebecca** *is holding it.*

*She shines it on* **Paul***, who is slumped on the ground.*

*She shines it on* **Helen**.

**Helen** *smiles*.

*She holds out the axe,* **Rebecca** *takes it*.

*Darkness*.

**Paul** *screams*.

## Day Five

### Seventeen

*Morning.*

*Lights rise at the wood shed. No one is there.*

*We hear the sound of birds.*

*We hear car doors closing.*

*We hear an engine starting.*

*We hear a car driving away.*

**End**